Colin Beale outside the South Porch at Old Blundell's. *The Times*, 1954.

THE MAKING OF AN ENGLISH PUBLIC SCHOOL

*For Pauline, Rachel,
Daniel and Ben.*

THE MAKING OF AN ENGLISH PUBLIC SCHOOL

by
M. J. W. Huggins

Preface by
A. R. B. Thomas, M.A.

Concluding chapter by
A. J. D. Rees, M.A.

PRO PATRIA POPULOQUE

"For all the things I learned at Blundell's
only two abode with me, and one of these was the
knack of fishing, and the other the art of swimming."

(From *Lorna Doone* by R. D. Blackmore)

Hiroona Publications, Spicery, Tedburn St. Mary, Devon.

© M. J. W. Huggins 1982

ISBN 0 9508183 0 5

Printed by Maslands Ltd., Tiverton, Devon.

CHAPTER LIST

Chapter		Page
1.	Peter Blundell and Popham	1
2.	Of Brass and Buildings	6
3.	The Masters 1601-1700	12
4.	The Masters 1700-1800	19
5.	The Masters 1800-1850	31
6.	A Tiverton School for Tiverton People	40
7.	Blackmore and Temple	45
8.	The Recovery—Rev. J. B. Hughes	54
9.	A. L. Francis	57
10.	From the Old to the New	63
11.	War	68
12.	"F"	80
13.	Rev. A. E. Wynne	84
14.	Rev. A. R. Wallace	93
15.	Rt. Rev. N. V. Gorton	99
16.	Rev. R. L. Roberts	104
17.	J. S. Carter	109
18.	Rev. J. M. Stanton	113
19.	A. C. S. Gimson	116
20.	Sport	122
21.	Customs and Traditions	136
22.	The Teaching Staff	146
	Conclusion—A. J. D. Ress—The Present and the Future	150

THE ILLUSTRATIONS

Plates:
Frontispiece: Colin Beale at Old Blundell's.

1. Mrs. Boulton engraving: Blundell's from the Tumbling Field.
2. Mrs. Boulton engraving: Blundell's from Copp's Court.
3. Frith drawing: Box beds in Old Blundell's.
4. Frith drawing: A boy's room in Old Blundell's.
5.—8. Some past Headmasters of Blundell's.
9. Parson Jack Russell.
10. Frederick Temple.
11. Memorial Tablet to Frederick Temple.
12. Memorial Tablet to R. D. Blackmore.
13. Blundell's Chapel before alterations.
14. The 1882 buildings today.
15. West window of Chapel.
16. Window of Lady Chapel.
17. Margaret Holman drawing: Big School.
18. Margaret Holman drawing: The Library.
19. Blundell's from Big Field: Before Chapel Extension.
20. Blundell's from the Big Field: After Chapel Extension.
21.—24. Some Old Blundellians who served in the First World War.
25. Front and reverse of Wills' Cigarette Card.
26. J. W. E. Hall and F. R. Clayton.
27. Professor Hill.
28. Captain P. F. Grenier.
29. Masters' Cricket XI.
30. Some F.H. Boys in the 1940's.
31. 1956 C.C.F. Inspection.
32. Queen Elizabeth the Queen Mother at Blundell's in 1967.
33. F.H. Play 1955 *Bats in the Belfry*.
34. N.C. Play 1982 *Romanoff and Juliet*.
35. The 1967 buildings.
36. A. R. B. Thomas and Miss Liddy Levo.
37. Miss Arabella Ashworth and Mr. Ian Whitehead.
38. The 1956 XV.
39. The 1981 Sevens winners.
40. The 1955 First XI.
41. The 1981 First XI.
42. The 1956 Bisley Team.
43. A strong F.H. XI in 1950.

44. Girls' Squash Team 1978.
45. Denny Dart of the U.S.A.
46. Senior Russell 1982.
47. Senior Russell 1982—Old Blundellian Challenge Race.
48. Vic Marks (F.H. 1968-73) Somerset and England.
49. Hugh Morris (W.) and Mr. Mepham of Gray Nicolls.

ILLUSTRATIONS IN TEXT

Page
5. Peter Blundell's signature.
11. Gateway to Old Blundell's: Mrs. Boulton.
16. "Bribed him with £150 to resign": Brian Newton.
18. Front view of Blundell's: Mrs. Boulton.
22. "Wedged between John Wesley and Mae West": Brian Newton.
30. Interior of Old Blundell's: Rudge.
39. Old School crest.
44. Interior of Old Blundell's: Rudge.
49. "Dear Mother, Temple's alright . . .": Brian Newton.
53. Old Blundell's: Illustrated London News.
58. Keats Medal.
60. Le vieux oncle Collé et tous: Brian Newton.
62. School crest.
67. Woodcut of School buildings.
92. The boy who walked in to the Common Room: G. L. Gettins.
98. Big School: Bryan De. Grineau.
103. Bisley practice: Bryan De Grineau.
108. "Burton J. should be higher": G. L. Gettins.
111. Definition of "agréable". G. L. Gettins.
121. La Fontaine's fables were really written by Aesop: G. L. Gettins.
124. ". . . Not letting his collaring . . . become feeble": Brian Newton.
143. The Lord High Warden of Croquet: Brian Newton.
145. Blundell's Squirrel.
149. From *Baby Baalamb gets into trouble:* M.H.
154. Hogarth engraving.
156. War Memorial pencil drawing by Dawn Cripps.

ACKNOWLEDGEMENTS

MY thanks are due to Sir John Palmer, Chairman of the Governors of Blundell's School for his kindly interest and encouragement, and to Mr. A. J. D. Rees, headmaster of Blundell's who allowed me access to the school, for his helpful suggestions concerning the publication of the book and for kindly undertaking to write the concluding chapter. I am indebted to Mr. J. B. Jenkins senior History master, for his generous help in giving such valuable bibliographical references whilst engaged in his own more scholarly history of the school. I would also wish to record my gratitude to my aunt Miss V. M. Huggins, who studied the manuscript and gave some most constructive criticism and helpful advice. I am very grateful indeed to Brian Newton for, at extremely short notice, drawing those delightful cartoons, and hope that we shall see much more of his work in other publications before long. I would like to thank Mrs. A. J. Gettins for kindly allowing me access to her late husband's amusing sketches. Mrs. Arabella Whitehead deserves a special word of thanks for bravely contributing her own recollections of being the first girl at Blundell's and I also appreciate very much the help and advice that Mr. Neate and Mr. May of Messrs. Maslands have given over the layout and design of the book.

I must also express my thanks to the following people who gave useful information and help:- The Librarian of the Devonshire Association; Mary Anne Bonney, Librarian of Punch; Major General J. G. Elliott C.I.E.; Alderman W. P. Authers, Messrs. C. L. Beale, E. R. Crowe, F. R. Clayton (who briefly emerged from a well earned retirement to correct my very rusty Latin), J. J. M. Street, C. M. Clapp, S. Marjoram, L. Flaws, H. R. Bayly, M. D. A. Bentata, T. I. Barwell, J. Edwards, R. C. A. Wellesley, B. Wood, Miss D. Bradbeer, and Miss Charlotte McKinnel and others. I would like to thank Mrs. Di Winslade and Miss Shirley Wilson those dedicated typists whose ability to decipher my strange hieroglyphics is frankly remarkable.

In Romans xii 8, Paul refers to a ministry of encouragement. I would like to pay particular tribute to my old Housemaster and friend A. R. B. Thomas (Bundy) who with his wife Liddy have given me so much encouragement and to whom I owe an overwhelming debt of gratitude; they have given me liberal access to the use of their own library, home and lunch table, and there is much in the book that is taken from Bundy's own comments and humour. I would also pay tribute to the encouragement given by our dear friends Nick and Alison Randall, who have so often urged me on. Finally I wish to record that without the love, encouragement and help I have constantly received from my wife Pauline this book would still be just a daydream.

PROLOGUE

"IN every situation . . . I have fallen into the habit of seeing what's wrong with it, not what's right with it. The good qualities, those things well done, are passed over quickly—in time scarcely noticed—in order to get on with the critique. All encounters in life, every personality, every institution and relationship is a mixture of the good and the bad. We habitually focus on the bad, we are training ourselves in negativism.

"We call it by other names. Looking with analytical eyes must surely be constructive, we tell ourselves, because what we're really asking is, 'How can such-and-such be improved?'

"But there is a secret cost in such an outlook to one's spiritual and mental health".

—Catherine Marshall: *Something More*

". . . if there is any excellence, if there is anything worthy of praise, think about these things."

St. Paul: *Letter to the Philippians (RSV)*

PREFACE

THIS book has come into being for various reasons. One is that Michael realises that the public schools are under attack, and thinks that someone should show what they have contributed to our country down the centuries. Another is that he has a very real love for his old school; this has inspired his research and his writing, but he worries that he has necessarily left out many people who have served his old school well. The last reason is that, fortunately for us, he fell from a haystack and wrote the book while recovering; had he not fallen, it is improbable that he would have had the time to spare from work on his farm outside Tedburn St. Mary.

Michael was at Blundell's from 1951-54, when he returned to work in Trinidad where his father was a clergyman. In time he married Pauline whose brother is Bishop of Chile, so it is no accident that he gives proper regard to the Christian tradition that has infused the life of the school for nearly four hundred years; indeed Christianity is at the heart of his own life.

Most of today's troubles are due to selfishness. Your schoolboy soon realises that self-centredness is unpopular, but he has a very long and difficult step to reach that love of God and love of one's neighbour, for which our Lord asked.

Finally, I should like to share Michael's wish that his book may give pleasure to many Old Blundellians.

A. R. B. Thomas

INTRODUCTION

FOR some time whilst doing the more mechanical farm jobs, I had toyed with the idea of illustrating a comparative book on some of the great English public schools giving short contrasting write-ups of their individual histories, customs and traditions. With the appropriate backer I had dreamed of visiting schools like Clifton, Uppingham, Oundle, Eton, Shrewsbury, Kelly, St. Paul's, King's, Bruton and so on. Whilst perhaps cultivating a field or dagging sheep I had visions of eventually producing something on the lines of 'Jane's Fighting Ships', but on public schools. Yet behind these lighthearted ramblings there was deep concern. Like many English traditions public schools seem to be under attack on two fronts; firstly that of sheer economics, and secondly, political dogmatism and bias. Since as far back as 1923, when George Bernard Shaw more than mildly suggested "that Eton, Harrow, Winchester . . . and their cheaper and more pernicious imitators should be razed to the ground and their foundations sown with salt", there have been repeated attacks on the Public School system, and in recent times these attacks have been led by very influential people from within more than one political party. There are over 250 public schools in Britian, many of which are as different from each other as chalk is from cheese; and probably Eton and Harrow themselves are very different to their general popular image or even to what they were like thirty years or so ago.

I will always remember with deep affection and gratitude my old school Blundell's, which I left over 27 years ago, and the thought of that fine old and often eccentric foundation being either razed to the ground or institutionalised into some kind of dull grey educational also-ran fills me with great sadness. Therefore, in an attempt to avoid the pitfalls of statistical averages and generalisations of this age, "The Making of an English Public School" has focused on aspects of the makings of this particular English public school, rather than on a bundle of obscure facts from several. Not the oldest, nor the largest, nor even amongst the most famous or exclusive, Blundell's is still very much an English public school of the finest tradition, with its own peculiar history and distinct atmosphere. It is one of the few old public schools to be actually named after its founder rather than after a town or religious institution. Much of the data in this book has been borrowed from other men's works, and in no way is it intended to replace the scholarly history at present being prepared by the senior History master at the school. Yet I hope that the various items I have collected together will give pleasure to all who love the old school and also give interest, appreciation and food for thought to others as to what lies behind some of these old communities generally classified for convenience sake as public schools.

1
Peter Blundell 1520-1601

"FOR Lorna's fortune I would not have, small or great, I would not have it; only if there were no denying, we would devote the whole of it to charitable uses, as Master Peter Blundell had done; and perhaps the future ages would endeavour to be grateful.". (From *Lorna Doone* by R. D. Blackmore).

The Will of Peter Blundell, Anno Domini 1599.

"In the Name of God Amen the nynth Day of June and the yeare of our Lord God 1599 and in the fortie one Yeare of the Reigne of our Sovereigne Lady Elizabeth by the Grace of God Queen of England Fraunce (sic) and Ireland Defender of the Faithe Ec I Peter Blundell of Tiverton in the Countie of Devonshire being wholl of Boddie and of good and perfecte Mynde and Memory Thanks be to almighty God remembering and weyinge the Uncertainty and Instabilitie of this mortal and transitory Lief and that every man borne into this Worlde as he is subjecte unto Deathe so is he uncertaine of Time Place and Manner wheare or by what Meanes the same shall happen unto him and myndeinge therefore the Pleasure of God and Quiett of Mynde to sett such Order and Staie for the Dispertion of such Landes Tenements Possessions Goodes Chattells Wares Plate Jewells ready Money and Depts whatsoever as it hath pleased Almighty God of his Goodness to give unto me in this Worlde as the same may be quietly enjoyed to those to whom I shall devise the same do therefore make ordeyne and declare this my last Will and Testament in Manner and Form followinge . . ."

So begins the Will of Peter Blundell, a long document carefully written out in Blundell's own handwriting when he was almost 80. How many of us today would be prepared to start our Wills with quite the same quality and style of preamble? Now a wealthy man, Peter Blundell was acknowledging that all he had came from God in the first place, and he therefore sought to fulfil his Christian stewardship by ensuring a careful dispersion of his wealth after his death, which he seemed to face with quiet confidence:

"First and before all things I commende and committ my Soule to Almightie God my Creator trusting most assuredly to be saved by the only Deathe Passion and Meritts of Jesus Christe beseeching the most blessed holy and most glorious Trinitie the Father and Sonne and the Wholy Goste three Parsons (sic) and one God to have Mercie upon me and to pardon and forgive mee all my Sinnes and that after this transitory Lief I may arycse with the Eleckte and be Partaker of Gods Glorie in the Kingdome of God and Lief everlasting . . ."

Peter Blundell was born in Devonshire in 1520, during the reign of Henry VIII, yet he was really an Elizabethan, a child of the Reformation, living at a time when some had received rather more than a mild roasting for their beliefs. Tradition has it that he was a poor lad who by sheer grit and determination rose to be a wealthy clothier, bringing his trade from Tiverton into London.

Having no direct descendants of his own, and being unmarried, Blundell was able, through the advice and direction of his dear and honourable friend Sir John Popham, Knight, Lord Chief Justice of England, to ensure that after his death in 1601 his fortune was not just redistributed through some generous bequests to dear friends, but devoted mainly to charitable purposes, including, for example, donations to various hospitals in London, such as Christ's Hospital, Newgate, St. Batholomew's Hospital and St. Thomas' Hospital, Southwark, and also grants to various trade guilds. Yet he was a man of no small vision, and his vision was to found a great school in his home town of Tiverton, not a small local school, but a great school. Although he was almost 80 when he painstakingly wrote out his Will, his mind was still very alert, and he could clearly picture the future school in fine detail.

"I will that my Executors . . . with all convenient speede upon a fytt and convenient Plott and piece of Grounde in Tyverton aforesaide by my Executors for the Purpose to be purchased and procured shall create and buyld a faier school house to conteyne for the place of teaching only in length one hundred foote and breadth fouer and twenty foote a Hawle Buttery and Kitchin all of convenient Space and Biggness to be joined into it with fit and convenient Roomes over the same Hawle Buttery and Kitchen all the windows well and strongly glassed and barred with iron barrs and well covered the Floor of the school to be well plancked with Plancks of oke supported and borne from the ground with strong hedges

or Beames with so many fitt and strong settles and Formes as shall be convenient having regarde to the business of the same schoole and Number of schollars to be taughte therein and to be divided on or neere the middal with some fit Partition of fower foot in height or there abouts yf it shal bea soe thoughte fitt and the schoole to be strongly wainscotted rounde abowte five or six foote above the settles . . ."

Blundell's eye for practical detail did not end at fixtures and fittings. He even instructed that the Masters be paid "Yearely for ever fiftie Poundes to be paide quarterly and the Usher twentie Markes (one Mark approximately 13/4d.)" This demonstrated tremendous foresight and wisdom. Fifty pounds per annum would mean that this school would be offering one of the most handsome salaries available at that time for any potential Headmaster in the country.

Years later in 1872, Dr. Frederick Temple, a former Blundellian then Bishop of Exeter, and later to become Archbishop of Canterbury, grasped this point when he wrote in a magnificent letter on educational reform to the Mayor of Exeter: "The whole difference between a truly great and very poor school, will depend on the sort of men that you put at the head." Peter Blundell was out to attract the best; but even then he had not quite finished. His Christianity was nothing nominal. He had lived during a time when matters of religion had hardly been settled after the Reformation. Again he made careful provision for the future:

"And for the increase of good and Godly Preachers of the Gospel my Will is that my Executors forthwith after my Deathe shall disburse and bestowe the some of twoe thousand powndes in and abowte the foundeing and establishinge six schollars to be students in Divinitie in the Universitie of Oxford or Cambridge or in both."

Peter Blundell died 9th May 1601. He was buried at St. Michael Pater Noster, London (later known as St. Michael Royal). His modest coat of arms are amongst those carved in the ancient Guildhall in Exeter, with the simple inscription underneath: 'Peter Blundell, Benefactor, 1599'. The following Latin Prayer has been said in the School since the foundation:

"Gratias agimus tibi, Domine Deus, quod nos hoc loco studii et pietatis et litterarum munificentia Petri Blundelli piae memoriae educamur. Teque rogamus pro summa tua misericordia, ut cum nos hoc tanto beneficio adjuti in laudem tui nominis perfecerimus, beatae resurrectionis aeternaeque felicitatis praemia consequamur, per Jesum Christum Dominum nostrum."

("We thank Thee, O Lord God, that through the bounty of Peter Blundell of pious memory we are being educated in this place of study, piety, and learning. And we beseech Thee of Thy exceeding mercy that when, assisted by this great benefit, we have profited to the praise of Thy name, we may obtain the rewards of a blessed resurrection and everlasting felicity, through Jesus Christ, Our Lord.")

Had Peter Blundell's Will read "Being wholl of Boddie and good and perfecte Mynde and Memory—I shall have spent every farthynge before I dye", Devon and England would have lost one of their wonderful heritages.

Sir John Popham proved his own good stewardship of the great trust that his old friend Blundell had placed in him. For "with all convenient speede" he certainly acted. Blundell died 9th May 1601, yet by the time his own beloved sovereign Queen Elizabeth I had died nearly two years later, Popham, on top of all his legal duties as Lord Chief Justice of England, was already building the School near the River Lowman. And the Foundation was maintaining seven scholars: John Berry and Christopher West at Balliol, and William Darant, John Pokingham, Thomas Pell, Richard Perrot and Lewis Land at Sidney Sussex. Blundell's was possibly the last great Elizabethan foundation.

Although Blundell had described in his Will almost exactly what he wanted for the School, from the personal to the technical, and it is very likely that the two friends spent happy hours discussing ways and means, Popham was still given a great deal of discretion in its execution. The building he had created did honour to the memory of his old friend. It stands today, said to be "the most perfect example of a Grammar School of the seventeenth century" (William Morris, 1834-1896), reflecting dignity and harmony in its design.

Popham divided up the Foundation Scholarhips between the universities. Two went to his old College, Balliol, Oxford, and two each to the new Colleges, Emmanuel and Sydney Sussex, Cambridge. Emmanuel, however, did not seem to come to terms, so the two scholars destined there were added temporarily to those of Sydney Sussex.

Popham died on 10th June, 1607. Born in 1531 in Somerset, he had led a distinguished career: M.P. for Bristol, Speaker of Parliament, Attorney General 1581-1592, (during the trial of Mary Queen of Scots in 1586), and Lord Chief Justice of England until his death, presiding at the historic trials of Sir Walter Raleigh and Guy Fawkes during that period. In 1606 Popham was instrumental in an attempt to found two English colonies in Virginia.

1. Blundell's School from the Tumbling Field.

2. Blundell's School from Copp's Court.

Both illustrations drawn and engraved on stone by Mrs. Boulton, wife of Dr. Anthony Boulton, Usher under Rev. Henry Sanders.

Drawings by Edward Blackstone Cockayne Frith, whilst a pupil 1845-47.

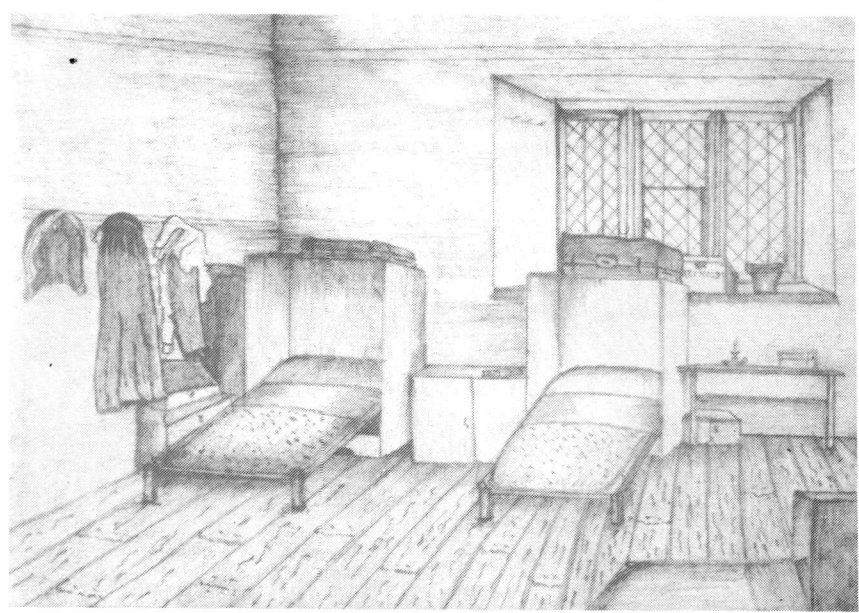

3. Box beds.

4. A boy's room at Old Blundell's.

Popham was unable to complete all the details of the Blundell's Trust, but his guiding hand had proved invaluable in the formation of a great School, where "a poor boy might find the means of rising to high destination and of doing honour to his school and to his town by his after life. By diligent use of the faculties that God had given him, without being beholden to anyone, the poor lad could obtain the aims of an honourable ambition". (Archbishop Frederick Temple)

Peter Blundell's signature

2
Of Brass and Buildings

THE great brass tablet that formerly was placed over the gateway at Old Blundell's, now transferred to the west wall of the Tower, has been, from time to time, a source of interest and debate. It contains two inscriptions, one in Latin and one in English.

> Hospita disquirens Pallas Tritonia sedem
> Est Blundellinae percita amore Scholae
> Ascivit sedem, placuit cupiensque foveri
> Hospes, ait, Petre sis qui mihi fautor eris.

> This free Grammar School
> was founded at the only
> cost and charge of Mr. Peter
> Blundell, of this town, sometime
> Clothier.

Anno Domini 1604

> Aetatis suae 81

Some authoritites claim that Popham had the inscription placed over the gate at the time of the foundation, and there could be truth in this, though other theories have been strongly advocated.

To the Editor,
The Blundellian, December 1st 1952
Sir,

I was most interested to read in your September number of the results of research by the Science and Classical Sixths into what is surely one of the School's greater mysteries. May I add some observations of my own?

The crude elegiacs of the Tower Inscription are even more than "inelegant"—they are downright bad. As they stand, they are clumsy and pedantic; they offend against elementary rules of prosody (where else would you find publicly displayed an elision in the second half of a pentameter, or a short vowel daring to stand before "*sch*olae"?). Again "percita" is hardly an Ovidian word, and the phrase "percita amore" as used of the Goddess of Learning, is in questionable taste!

It is surely inconceivable they could have been the work of a Headmaster. They can only have been the work of a boy—and that too of no very accomplished versifier. They compare most unfavourably with Milton's school-boy efforts of the same date, and would have earned a flogging for an Eton or Westminster boy two centuries later! How they can have been preserved as they have been must remain a mystery. There must have been a very special reason, once. (Perhaps they were the best effort of our original Classical Sixth, the first in the West Country).

Incidentally, I am sure the inscription never read "Petrus qui," which omits a main verb, and thus gives no sense at all. I would suggest Prince misread his m.s. note "Petre sis," and Dunsford copied him, without reference to the original.

While at the School last Summer, I knocked off a fairly literal translation in English Elegiacs—a "barbarous experiment" intended (if no more) to reproduce the barbarity of the Latin:-
"Sojourner, seeking about for a home, Tritonian Pallas
Lighting on Blundell's School, greatly was smit with desire,
Knew her abode, was gladdened, and, eager aye to be cherished,
'Peter,' she said, 'Be my host—ever my patron to be'."
(There is some play on the double meaning of 'hospes', both 'host' and 'guest').

In any case, the meaning is clear—"Classical Learning found no place in the West, till the founding of Blundell's. Here it throve from the first—and may it continue to flourish." And, with all due deference to our eminent Scientists, may "Pallas of the Triton Lake" ever find her due place in our School!

The great fact remains, commemorated truly in these "inelegant" lines—Peter Blundell founded a seat of Learning without equal in the hitherto uncultured West, and his work abides.

Yours, etc.,
R. S. Chalk.
St. Philip's Parsonage, Weston Mill, Plymouth.

23rd March 1953.

The Editor, Blundellian,

Sir,

I have read with much interest Mr. Chalk's letter about the Tower elegiacs, and should like to break a lance with him. That they are bad, horribly bad, we may agree. But surely that makes it inconceivable that they should *not* have been the work of a Headmaster? Who else would have been allowed to perpetuate such an abomination, and get away with it? Who else could have had such lines graven in brass, to be handed down to future ages? Who else would have been allowed to picture a maiden lady of *very* uncertain age, "cupiens foveri", addressing our pious Founder familiarly by his Christian name, and proposing to billet herself upon him for an indefinite period? Is it not inconceivable that the Headmaster of the period would not have censored those lines out of existence, if they had not been of his own composition?

> I remain, Sir,
> Yours etc.,
> G. B. Crosthwaite.
> Browns Town,
> Jamaica.

There have been various translations of the Latin, one of the better ones perhaps, being by Thomas Wood, a former Blundellian and Usher, 1760-1788.

> "Minerva on her travels sought to find
> Some hospitable seat to please her mind,
> She saw this school—struck with the stately dome,
> She cried with transport 'This shall be my home.'"

Another translation quoted by Martin Dunsford in 1790:-

> "When wand'ring Pallas sought sweet retreat
> In Blundell's School at length she fixed her seat.
> 'Peter', she said, beneath thy roof I'll rest,
> And at thy table sit a well pleased guest'."

William Kiddell, in his poem 'Tiverton' 1757, really goes to town on the theme of wandering goddesses setting up camp at Blundell's.

> "... The Goddess heard his vow,
> And swore by Him who maked the Mountains bow,
> The same should flourish in eternal Youth,
> Preserv'd by Her, by Phoebus, and by Truth.

Then quick descending from the Etherial Bow'rs,
Where blooms eternal spring, and never-fading Flow'rs,
She rose resplendent to his dazzl'd sight,
As mild as May, as glitt'ring as the Light:
And smiling said—'O Blundell, this thy Dome
Shall vie with Athens, or Politer Rome;
And here conspicuous will I fix my seat,
And leave dull Pedants to harangue the Great;
From Faction, Criticks, and the World's false Noise,
Here dwell secure, and nought disturb my Joys;
Here thirst of knowledge shall the Youth inspire
To read a Virgil with a Virgil's Fire,
                                               . . . etc.

All this is a terrible libel on Peter Blundell, a practical man of the Reformation, who would have given any wandering Goddess very short shrift—and he certainly made no provision in his Will for any. John Heathcote and Company would have been better employed evicting Goddesses than boarders in 1847.

During the latter part of the nineteenth century, a competition was arranged whereby a prize of a sovereign was offered for the best English rendering of the brass tablet's Latin. The prize was not awarded, however, as none of the entries was considered to be of sufficient merit, yet the following amplified and highly irreverent version was a product of that competition:

"Where are you going to, my pretty maid?
I am seeking a home for myself, she said.
And where do you come from, my pretty maid?
From the Lacus Tritonis, Sir, she said
And pray, fair lady, where may that be?
'Tis an academical pleasantrie,
Meaning Girton College, Cantabrigiae,
And where is your fortune, my pretty maid?
My learning's my fortune, sir, she said,
I was first in the list of Wranglerie,
I was senior in Classics pre-eminentlee,
Which I think, you will allow was a goodly degree.
I am Scient: et Art: et Medicinae.
Et Legum, Doctrixque Philosophiae.
Then all you want is the £. s. d.
And you just for men the D.D, said he.
(I am charmed to the heart with this acadamee;

>Such a home to attain would fill me with glee,
>I long to be petted, aside said she.)
>Now prithee, fair Sir, thy name tell me.
>Peter Blundell, my name, at your service, said he.
>Then be thou my hee-hum-host, Peter Blundell, said she,
>For I see you'll take care of me properlee."

Martin Dunsford (a pupil at Blundell's 1752-1757) describes the school he knew:

"The noble edifice, somewhat resembling the colleges of the Universities, is situated at the east end of the town, on the south side of the road leading to Cullompton, near the banks of the Lowman, which runs close to the wall of the garden towards the west. It is a strong stone building, having a durable roof of chestnut wood, built similar to that of Westminster Hall, and covered with blue slate. The walls are about 3 feet thick, and 18 feet high; and the top of the roof 36 feet from the floor.

"The whole is a regular structure, about 170 feet long and 30 feet wide; divided in length into three parts; separated by two passages, having two arched stone porches before them, each about 15 feet square without. Three large stone windows are uniformly placed in the front of each division, and one in each porch. The front of the whole pile towards the North is neatly cased with yellow Purbeck stone, and exhibits an elegant and magnificent appearance. The eastern passage, 7 feet wide, enclosed by strong oak railings, leads to the Ushers' apartments, and separates the Schools. On the left is the higher school, where the Master himself presides. The higher school is 51 feet long and 24 feet wide, well floor'd with oak, having strong ranks of forms of thick oak plank on each side. At the upper end is a desk for reading prayers, and a very large window behind it; another window on the south side, and three towards the north, in front. At the south-east corner is a doorway to the closet or study for the Master. On this side of the gallery is the face of the clock. Under it, and over the doorway, carved in the timber, P.B. 1604.

"The Lower School is on the right of the passage, and under the care of the Usher. It is 48 feet long and 24 wide, well floored also with oak, and having two strong ranks or forms of thick oak plank on each side. At the upper end is a similar desk to that in the Lower School, Behind it, in the wall is a niche, supposed to have been intended for a statue of the Founder. At the south-west corner is a door-way to the Master's apartments; one window towards the south, and three towards the north in front. On this side the gallery, over the doorway, is also carved in timber P.B. 1604. Both Schools are wainscotted six feet high from the floor.

"Over the passage is a gallery leading from the porch chamber to the upper rooms of the Ushers' house. Above the gallery, in the centre of the roof, between the Schools, is an elegant lead turret, or cupola, a pleasing external ornament, in which is a large bell for the clock, and to summon the boys to school etc. The bell was first hung in the cupola in April, 1613, the present bell was placed there in 1787.

"The porch-way on the west leads to the Master's dwellinghouse. On the right is a spacious dining-hall, with a large convenient parlour at the west end, both together of equal dimensions with one of the schools; over these are the best lodging rooms. In this hall is a very large painting of the School house etc. by one of the boys, and in the parlour are preserved good paintings of the Masters, Saunders, Rayner, Smith, Daddo, Atherton and Keates; another of Rayner; a lesson painting of Keates, a very good likeness; and a small print of Wesley.

"From the Hall is a passage to the kitchen and other offices contiguous; over which also are numerous lodging rooms. Behind are large courtyards, convenient outhouses, a rich meadow, orchard and gardens. In front of the School is a fine level quadrangular field, or green, about an acre, surrounded by a well built stone wall about 10 feet high, coped with yellow Purbeck stone: within a row of twenty-six lime trees, planted about ten feet from the walls which form a shady summers walk.

"The whole of the premises, including the green, occupy a space of about 4 acres. The green measures exactly one acre of land within the lime trees . . ." Mr. Blundell directed the whole plan in his Will and determined the dimensions of the several departments.

The Gateway to Old Blundell's.—Mrs. Boulton

3
The Masters

Joseph Hall 1601. "The Headmaster for half a day."

HALL was born 1st July 1574 near Ashby-de-la-Zouch. He rose to fame as an "English Bishop (Exeter and Norwich), moralist, controversialist and satirist, a notable figure in Literature in his own right, and as an opponent of Milton and of some importance in the history of ideas both as a churchman and as a moral philosopher." (*Encyclopaedia Brittanica*.) He died 8th September 1656.

Hall was about 27 and a fellow of new and strongly puritan Emmanuel College, Cambridge when, in 1601, Dr. Lawrence Chaderton, the first Master of Emmanuel (and one of the translators of the Bible) recommended him to Popham, who offered him the mastership of Blundell's. Hall accepted but on "coming away from the Judge in the street, a messenger delivered a letter, tendering the Rectory of Halstead, earnestly desiring Hall to accept it . . . such was evidently his desire." Hall sought Dr. Chaderton's advice, and his advice was that Hall was really bound to the acceptance of Blundell's School, but Hall was not persuaded, and recorded the occasion himself as follows:

"The Doctor only pleaded the distaste which would thereupon be justly taken by the Lord Chief Justice, whom I undertook fully to satisfie, which I did with no great difficulty, commending to his Lordship in my room my old Friend and Chamber-fellow, Mr. Chulmley."

The Rev. Hugh Chulmley or Chomley. "The Headmaster who never taught." c. 1601-1604.

There appears to have been some debate as to whether or not Hugh Chulmley could be strictly termed Master of Blundell's, as there seems to

The Lord Chief Justice
Sir John Popham

Joseph Hall Bishop of Exeter and Norwich
First Headmaster of Blundell's

William Daddo
Headmaster 1740-1757

Philip Atherton
Headmaster 1757-1775

The Rev. Richard Keats, M.A.
Headmaster 1779-1797

Dr. William Page Richards
Headmaster 1797-1823

Dr. Alldersey Dicken, D.D.
Headmaster 1825-1833

Archdeacon Henry Sanders
Headmaster 1834-1847

J. B. Hughes
Headmaster 1847-1873

A. L. Francis
Headmaster 1873-1917

Rev. A. E. Wynne
Headmaster 1917-1930

The Very Rev. A. R. Wallace
Headmaster 1930-1934

The Rt. Rev. N. Gorton
Headmaster 1934-1943

The Rev. R. L. Roberts, C.V.O.
Headmaster 1943-1947

J. S. Carter
Headmaster 1948-1959

The Rev. J. M. Stanton
Headmaster 1949-1971

be evidence that he resigned to take up a living at Tiverton before he ever taught.

The Tiverton Historian A. S. Mahood (DB 1913-1915) quotes a letter written by a later Master, George Hume (1669-1681). "Mr. Chulmley some time Canon of your Church (Exeter) was the first Schoolmaster elected, but I never heard that he taught in the school. Yet he taught somewhere else and received the stipend for some time."

The Rev. Chulmley preached at some of the very early Old Boy day services, according to the great account book, in 1618, 1620, 1621, and 1622.

Samuel Butler. (c. 1604-1647)

Butler was Headmaster for about 43 years. He brought with him to the School several gentlemen's sons as boarders, so that his scholars were not only local. One of his pupils was George Bull, later Bishop of St. David's. A contemporary biography of Bull's refers to Samuel Butler as "very eminent in his profession, an excellent grammarian, both for Latin and Greek, diligent in his office and vigilant in his care and observation of his scholars." Butler must have had some anxious moments in 1612, for most of Tiverton was burnt in a magnificent fire that left only the Castle, St. Peter's Church, the School and a few houses.

Butler was still Master when, after the Battle of Nazeby had been fought, Fairfax sent Major General Massey ahead to survey Tiverton, which was still very much in Royalist hands. Massey made Mr. Blundell's School his headquarters, and ordered batteries to be raised against the Church and Castle. When Fairfax followed, there were now two Parliamentary Generals and six or eight Colonels sitting in the School House. Within two days of Fairfax's arrival, the Castle was taken. These events must have been quite a source of excitement and disruption for the boys. Although in the following years there appeared to be frequent entries in the School account book "Mending School House", it is very unlikely that these dilapidations were connected at all with the General, who the following year, on entering the surrendered Oxford, immediately placed a strong guard to protect the Bodleian library.

Two of Butler's pupils in particular suffered heavily in the Royalist cause. Peter Sainthill, who was born in 1593, a Colonel in the Royal Ranks, lost his Bradninch Estate after the fall of Exeter. Although as M.P. for Tiverton he had accepted the need for reform, he would not stomach the taking up of arms against the Lord's annointed. He died an exile in Italy aged 45.

The other Blundellian who should be mentioned here is the Rev. Richard Newte. Newte left Blundell's in 1628, and was a fellow of Exeter College, Oxford. He succeeded Hugh Chulmley as Rector of Clare (this was one of the four Portions controlled by St. Peter's, Tiverton) in 1641. In 1646 he and his family were grossly ill-treated and thrown out of his Tidcombe Rectory which was burned by the local Parliamentary supporters. The Newtes were left destitute, and even forced to lodge several nights in the open in a wood. In present times, when we are encouraged to demand our 'rights' it is interesting to study Newte. He was a man of the cloth who appeared to take note of injunction in Matthew v. 44, and returned during the period several times to preach to the plague-stricken Tiverton, and, at the risk of his life, to tend people in their own houses, where they were dying at the rate of 250 a week. His living was restored to him in 1660, and he was made a Chaplain to Charles II, but when the King offered him the Deanery of Exeter, he declined, for he preferred to remain a country parson.

Incidentally Blundell's educated five successions of Newtes of Tidcombe Rectory. The first had been a schoolboy before the Mayflower sailed, and the last of them left the Rectory after the United States of America had become a separate nation. Some of their Memorials may be seen in St. Peter's Church, Tiverton.

The name Newte still remains with the School. Richard Newte generously donated an exhibition for local boys, and the first year's under 14 Rugby XV is called *The Newtes*. Newtes Hill, near Tiverton, is second only to Porlock Hill as the steepest drive in the West Country.

Henry Osborne (1648-1651).

Very little is known about this man, but his Headship was during the time of the Commonwealth. Like the legendary Vicar of Bray, perhaps he kept quiet and careful for good reason.

Henry Batten (1651-1669).

The old custom of Oak Apple Day on May 29th would have commenced during Batten's period.

The School was made to resemble a 'veritable forest' as a contemporary writer puts it: "In memory of the escape and restoration of Charles the second, who, when pursued by a portion of that army which afterwards dethroned and beheaded his father Charles the first, eluded his pursuers by climbing a large oak tree and concealing himself amid its branches, all of which you will find recorded in *The History of England*."

The boys used to rise very early that day and scour the countryside armed with axes, saws and possibly certain unmentionable weapons in order to cut great strips of oak foliage from hedgerows and trees in the surrounding countryside. Quite predictably local farmers did not always take kindly to this behaviour. Later in 1883 eleven Blundell's boys were surrounded by "the minions of the local farmers, who held them in durance vile in a barn until the messenger they had despatched of their number had brought back the ransom of a shilling a captive." An account of Blundell's in the 1830's gives the atmosphere:

"The Upper School was decorated with oak, and transformed into a veritable forest, in the recess of which we boys arranged ourselves as best we could, the climax which all this foreshadows, being the recitation by each boy in the Upper School, of a piece of poetry, the selection of which was quite unfettered, if only a length of some 20 lines at least was attained.

"The lofty schoolroom lent itself readily to our rude but vigorous decoration. The final effort (Finis coronat opus) was the selection of a branch that was to form a sort of canopy, under which the subsequent performance was to take place. Some one was found who was cunning to throw a stone; this with a string attached, was cast over the old beams, (spoils of the Invincible Armada, as we believed them to be); the branch aforesaid was then made fast and the lower part was then decorated with flowers; it was hoisted up and left to hang some six feet above the floor. The huge branch was cunningly dropped on the head of the last boy at the end of his recitation, unless he managed more cleverly to evade it. At 11 o'clock (if we remember aright) the Head Master solemnly entered, and the proceedings began, the boys coming forward according to their seniority in the School. The actual "speaking" or recitation was, as might be expected, of unequal merit: to some, especially the beginners, it was very nervous work, and the fateful moment was much dreaded when we had to emerge from our leafy bower and take our stand under the improvised canopy, first placing the "book of words" on the Masters' desk. As a rule there was no "break down", we got through our task nervously or otherwise. Once (only once) we recall the fate of a youngster, who had essayed to learn Wallers lines on the rose, beginning "Go, lovely rose", Three times he began, each time only getting as far as the above exordium, when at last (the patience of the Master being exhausted), the book was summarily returned, with the obvious, if peremptory comment 'Go, lovely Rose.' "

Temple records the same custom in his day and tells us that the most popular piece was the burial of Sir John Moore. "According to tradition it was said 26 times at least, and the hero was committed to the earth not silently but amid tumultuous applause."

Cricket generally followed in the afternoon, and the day was wound up with games or sports.

George Hume (Master 1669-1684.)

Hume is best remembered by the delicate and amusing incident when the Feoffees (Trustees of the School), bribed him with £150 to resign, as he was then 90. It would have been during his mastership that Blackmore's Jan Ridd, hero of *Lorna Doone*, would have attended the School.

"Here by the time I was twelve years old, I had risen into the upper School, and could make bold with Eutropius and Caesar—by aid of our English version—and as much as six lines of Ovid. Some even said that I might, before manhood, rise almost to the third form, being of a persevering nature; albeit, by full consent of all (except my Mother), thick headed. But that would have been, as I now perceive, an ambition beyond a farmers' son; for there is but one form above it, and that made of masterful scholars, entitled rightly 'monitors'. So it came to pass, by the grace of God, that I was called away from learning, whilst sitting at the desk of the junior first in the upper school, and beginning the Greek verb τύπτω.

"My eldest grandson makes so bold to say that I never could have learned φιλέω, ten pages further on, being all he himself could manage, with plenty of stripes to help him . . ."

J. R. Viles (Milestones 1971-1975, S. S. Exhibitioner) more than earned his Mahood Essay prize in 1974, when he virtually audited the Great Account Book of Blundell's 1670-1679, a period during the time of Hume.

Viles brought to light some intriguing facts such as that a certain Leonard Farmer used 19,450 nails repairing the School in one year, charging £7 for his work, or that the mending of the gate was a yearly task and that on average a varying assortment of seven locks and keys were mended or replaced annually. His account of the Old Boys feasts of that time is especially worth repeating.

"A source of endless enjoyment to the Governors of the School must have been the particularly frequent feasts held in their honour every year. In fact, there seems to have been a trader in Tiverton, a certain James Clarke, who specialised in providing every necessity for a dinner in the realms of servants, horses, and most important of all, liquid refreshment. The beginnings of this pleasurable practice were somewhat unspectacular. In 1670 a mere 9 bottles of ordinary wine were purchased, along with 2/- worth of beer and the hire of one servant. The event suddenly became more alcoholic a year later, until in 1677 the following bill was received by the Treasurer-

for 34 ordinaires at 24d.	£3. 8. 0.
for 59 ordinaires at 12d.	2. 19. 0.
for 2 dozen ½ of Canary at 24d.	3. 0. 0.
for 3 dozen ½ of Sherry at 18d.	3. 3. 0.
for 3 dozen of Clarett at 12d	1. 16. 0.
for beere, for tobacco and pipes.	11. 0.
for horse meat.	6. 0.
	£15. 3. 0.

"Such a bill was worthy of a seal and the signature on the receipt was witnessed by two independent people. Economies had, however, been made on the more unnecessary items. Sugar, servants and horses are all missing from the account, whereas on previous occasions they had always appeared. Maybe it is a sign of increasing affluence that all the Feoffees now owned horses, so that the only job left to James Clarke was to provide drink for them, and of course, feed their horses. But assuming that Stuart horses were not carniverous—an assumption repudiated by the scene between Ross and the Old Man in *Macbeth*—and assuming that the Governors had not suddenly taken a liking for horse meat—they never took it before or after 1677—the situation becomes increasingly perplexing. Looking back through previous records, however, it soon becomes apparent that the item 'oats and hay' normally occured in the position taken by this enigmatic 'horse meat'. One can only speculate that perhaps the Governors were feeling particularly benevolent on that October night, and that perhaps James Clarke was rewarded with a little liquid for his labours."

John Sanders (Master 1684-1698).

Sanders was the first of three Old Blundellian Headmasters, the other two being John Jones (Master 1733) and Dr. Aldersey Dicken (1823-1843). He was a fellow of Sidney Sussex.

It was during the Headship of Sanders that Martin Dunsford makes the first record of Blundell's boys rowing in tubs raided from the local brewery when the Lowman and Exe had flooded.

4
The Masters 1700-1800

William Rayner (Master 1698-1730).

"Skilled in all Tongues, see Rayner treads the stage,
Severe his virtue, awful in his age,
While others follow all the musty Rules
Of barb'rous Monks, or slow phlegmatic Fools,
From ev'ry Weed, lo! Rayner clears the Ground,
And in his Grammar all the Man is found!"

(William Kiddell).

WILLIAM Rayner was the first of the Westminster-educated Head Masters, and by repute, one of the best Headmasters of Blundell's. Martin Dunsford (1790) comments:

". . . He (Rayner) is said to have been skilled in classic learning, an excellent Master, and remarkable for strict discipline. The School flourished so much in his time, that an assistant master became necessary to him in the higher school. Many respectable scholars were bred well under his tuition. He died in the Masters' apartment at the School House, after an attentive service of 32 years, and was buried in the chancel of St. Peter's Church, Tiverton."

Among the "respectable scholars" under Rayner, were names like Captain Atkins, Lord Annesley, Mr. Crab, Sir Matthew Day, Lord St. Ledger, Ed. Dyke, Esq., and Sir John Carew. John Conybere (1692-1755) became Bishop of Bristol and Thomas Haytor (1702-1762) became Bishop of Norwich and London and tutor to the sons of Frederick, Prince of Wales. Another famous pupil of Rayner was Bampfylde Moore Carew (1693-1758). Carew never actually became a Bishop, but ran away from Blundell's in about 1708. Carew, who was from a very old and respected West Country family, after a most unorthodox and adventurous career, was to become King of the Gypsies. It would appear that the reason Carew 'eloped' was that having started a pack of hounds with some fellow Blundellians, one day followed them at the gallop through several fields of standing corn. Unfortunately Devon farmers have never really taken kindly to such behaviour, and very severe retribution seemed on the way.

The keeping of hounds near the School probably became one of those traditions that continued on the quiet.

John Russell, who entered Blundell's in 1809 seemed to lead as full a life at School as he did in later years when he was known affectionately as Parson Jack Russell, the famous hunting Devonshire cleric, breeder of a type of hunting terrier dog and sporting friend of the Prince of Wales.

Whilst a junior at Blundell's, Russell set his ferrets on a monitor's rabbits as a reprisal for bullying. Russell was severely flogged for this by the then Headmaster, Dr. Richards, who used a heavy whalebone riding crop as the instrument of displeasure. As his schooling advanced, bored with just ferreting, Russell secretly kept a pack of hounds at an outlying farm, sharing joint mastership with a fellow pupil, Bob Bovey. When Richards got scent of this, Russell very narrowly escaped expulsion.

Despite his sporting deviations, Russell showed that he was also a fair classical scholar, gaining a £30 Exhibition to Exeter College, Oxford, but immediately blew the first instalment of his Blundell's bounty on a horse which, alas, turned out to be a dud. At Oxford Russell proved to be an excellent boxer, having already had good experience in the ironing box at Blundell's, (that triangular area of grass between the porches of Old Blundell's where Jan Ridd fought Robin Snell in *Lorna Doone*) and appeared to enjoy some tough bouts in the ring. It was in later years that Russell admitted to the then elderly Dr. Richards that Richards was the only man that he was ever afraid of. "I've set to with some of the hardest men in England, and never found one who could hit like you".

Russell was not the only pupil that Dr. Richards had cause to severely flog over the question of livestock. Thomas Bury Wells, who entered Blundell's in 1806 with a fellow pupil, Phil Lardner, "in the days of short commons and hard living angled and caught a duck at the back of the School. The duck was quickly plucked and put into a pie before it was missed. An old woman, however, finding that her duck was missing, and having heard that Mother Denham had made duck pie for the boys, petitioned Dr. Richards, and swore to the duck."

9. Rev. John Russell (Parson Jack Russell).

10. The Most Rev. Frederick Temple, Archbishop of Canterbury.

11. Frederick Temple.   12. R. D. Blackmore.

Memorial Tablets to Frederick Temple and R. D. Blackmore, Exeter Cathedral.

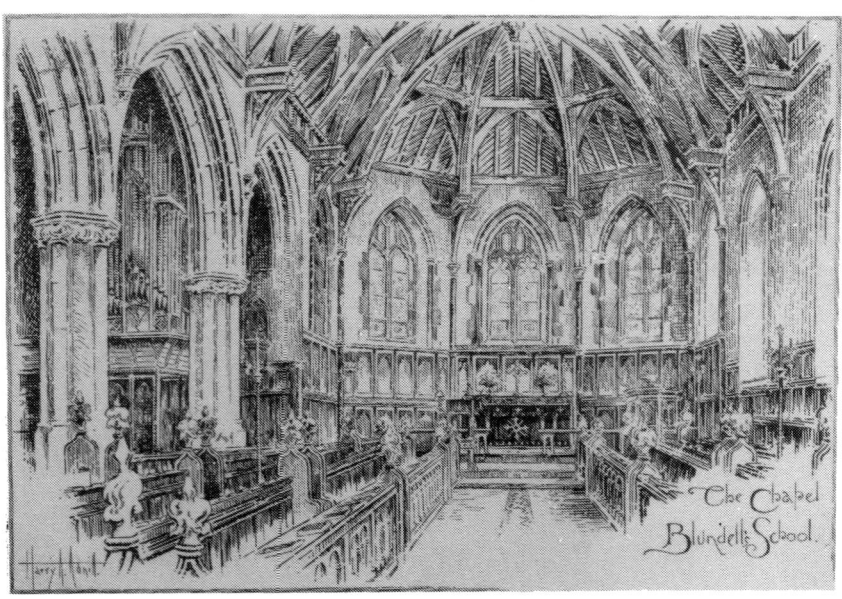

13. Blundell's School Chapel, before alterations.

The tradition of eccentric livestock activities and affection for birds amongst the pupils at Blundell's, seems to have continued throughout the years. There was once an Assistant Chaplain at Blundell's in the early part of this century who often had to slip his surplice over his hunting gear as he rushed to Chapel after a quick morning's gallop. E. A. Horniman (F.H. 1941-1944) kept an owl in his study, whilst ten years later Hill G. (F.H. 1951-1956) kept a buzzard in number one study. This bird was fed on small game, and Hill was even known to smuggle his meat ration out of the Dining Hall to feed the bird—quite a sacrifice for a 16-year old in those austere days, when Miss Autumn was able to perform miracles in the Dining Hall, assisted by "Grandpa" and "Spiv". The birds last seen gracing the walls of that particular study did not, however, have feathers.

Samuel Smith (Master 1730-1732).

"Smith next, who with inimitable Art,
Tempers the Master with the Parent's Part;
Lures the young Mind his precepts to regard
And makes ev'n Learning be its own Reward." (Kiddell)

Dunsford comments that Samuel Smith, A.M. (Trinity Oxford) "came from Crewkerne in Somersetshire, and added many boys to the School that had been under his care in that place, so that probably the boys were more numerous during the time Mr. Smith officiated than at any other period (up to 1770). He was a good Master, an amiable and benevolent man; several instances of his humane attention to the distressed are recorded. He published, in the year 1732, an account of the great fire in Tiverton in 1731, at which calamitous time his friendly aid was beneficial."

This was now the second time since the foundation that a disastrous fire had hit Tiverton.

John Jones (Master 1733).

Jones, ever gentle, moulds the Soul with Ease,
Born to instruct, and only lives to please.

(Kiddell)

Jones, a fellow of Balliol, was the second Old Blundellian Headmaster of the School, though he was only Master for a few months. Apparently he died in office.

Samuel Wesley (Master 1733-1739).

He was the son of the Rev. Samuel Wesley, who is remembered in the *Penguin Dictionary of Quotations,* wedged between John Wesley (one of his sons), and Mae West.

... wedged between John Wesley and Mae West

Samuel junior was the elder brother of John Wesley, and Charles Wesley—and also of another 16 brothers and sisters as well. He was born in 1690 and entered Westminster School in 1704, becoming a Queen's Scholar in 1707, too late to have been under Dr. Richard Busby, that great classical scholar and flogger, who died in 1695. From Westminster he went to Christ Church, Oxford, returning to his old School as senior Usher in 1714, a post he held for 20 years, teaching there at one time his younger brother Charles.

Wesley was extremely disappointed when he was passed over for the vacant Headmasterhsip of Westminster in 1732. There could have been several reasons for this. Wesley had become a brilliant satirist, and had made some scathing attacks on the Whigs and Walpole. He had been a close friend of men like Harley, Earl of Oxford, Addison, Dean Swift and Prior, and especially Bishop Francis Atterbury, who was banished for plotting against King George I in 1722. The Trustees of Westminster may have been embarrased at the thought of such a man becoming Master; however, the reason given was that it was because he was married. A year later, through the influence of the second Earl of Oxford, Wesley was appointed Headmaster of Blundell's School instead.

Dunsford, in his history of Tiverton, sums up the enigma of Wesley as a Headmaster:

"Different parties have given this Master a very different character, by one he is represented to have been scrupulously conscientious, of great integrity and benevolence, and to have possessed a pleasing simplicity of manner; by others, as rigorous, haughty, unsociable and bigoted."

One of the 'others' was Kiddell, who made no bones about his own views of Wesley (this, by the way is the Goddess still speaking:

"Wesley alone (curst with excessive Pride)
Wesley alone shall want me for a Guide.
To him I leave dry puns in Scales to poize,
And wield a Birch, the terror of all Boys."

Possibly Wesley missed the intellectual stimulation of his old London set of Swift and his friends and found the company of Devon squires somewhat dull in comparison. Also his health was none too good, though he loved the Devon scenery around Old Blundell's.

"Without are beauteous prospects seen,
Gardens and river, hills and green;
Within my books at will supply,
Delightful, useful company."

It was while he was at Blundell's that Wesley decided to publish the first edition of his poetical works (1736) which he openly admitted to be for "the profit proposed by the subscription" rather than for their excellence. Yet his work has been recognised and praised by the poet Robert Southey, and in the grammar prefixed to his great Dictionary, Dr. Samuel Johnson quotes Wesley's *Epitaph on an Infant* as the best specimen of a certain kind of poetry.

The number of pupils attending Blundell's rose by 40 during Wesley's Headship; but that was not the only thing that was increased. He also increased the School fees.

"I've alarmed the country round
By raising board to twenty pound,
Huge provocation, I confess,
So great it never will be less.
Poor Saunders drudged incessant here
The larger part of twenty year,
What riches did his kindred find?
He left his victor plate behind.
Full thirty years has Rayner Stay'd,
Rayner, oft praised, but never paid!
His boarders though so gainful thought,
Cost hundreds more than ere they brought."

There is no record of John Wesley actually visiting his elder brother at Blundell's, but Charles Wesley stayed at the School in 1737 when he returned from Georgia. When Samuel Wesley his father died, his mother joined him and his beloved wife 'Nutty' at the School, He died in office on 6th November 1739, he is buried and there is a Memorial to him at St. George's Church, Tiverton.

"A finished classical scholar, a poet, and a devout man, but he was never reconciled to the Methodism of his brothers."

(Encyclopaedia Britannica).

William Daddo (Master 1740-1757)

"See Daddo now, Minerva's favorite son
Compleats the work that Jones has just begun.
Of manners mild, he scorns the Fasces' aid.
Great in his genius, in his Temper Stay'd;
Partial to none, yet lov'd alike to all
His works shall praise him—thousands weep his fall."

(Kiddell).

This time it seems to be a mystical Goddess who is being libelled by Kiddell, for Minerva—or Pallas Athene—being a virgin goddess, is not normally credited with having a favourite son.

Martin Dunsford was a scholar of Daddo's, so his comments on the man are particularly interesting. He records that Daddo was a Cornishman who became a fellow of Balliol. "He was esteemed a good classic scholar, and an attentive Master. The boys were so numerous during a great part of his time, as to make an assistant Master necessary in the Higher School. His good temper, easy manners and social turn made his company desirable." Rather a nice thing to say about one's old Headmaster.

Daddo took a kindly interest in a promising boy from Totnes, taking him into his house, educating him and finally sending him to Oxford, where he became a very distinguished Hebrew scholar. His name was Benjamin Kennicot.

Another of Daddo's pupils was Richard Beardon, who also led a distinguished career, becoming Master of Jesus' College Cambridge (when a fellow of St. John's), and Tutor to George III's nephew, Prince William Frederick, afterwards Duke of Gloucester. Bearden was made Bishop of Gloucester in 1789, and Bishop of Bath and Wells in 1802. Yet another of Daddo's pupils was John Davey (1732-1798). A native of Tiverton and the first holder of a Blundell's 'Newte' Exhibition, Davey was Master of Balliol. L. T. Rendell, in the chapter he wrote on John Davey in Blundell's Worthies, points out that a man like Davey lived in memorable times. "The Rebellion of '45 broke out when he was a boy at School. He was graduate of Oxford when the reign of George III began. In middle life he knew of the revolt of the American Colonies and the momentous *Declaration of Independence*. Later still, during the years of his Mastership, occurred the French Revolution, and its sequel, the overthrow of an ancient Monarchy."

The poet Robert Southey, who matriculated at Balliol when Davey was Master, wrote this amusing sketch:

"I go, God save me,
To Doctor Davey
Of Balliol College Head,
And when he came,
My own sweet name
In modest manner said
Dear Tom, his whig
Is not so big
As many Doctors more,
And so I may
Presume to say,
His Wisdom is the more."

Daddo must have been very grateful to his predecessor, Wesley, for raising Blundell's boarding fees, for he retired in 1757 a very wealthy man. It was during the time of Daddo that in 1750 John Wesley came to preach at Tiverton. It was at the time of an Old Boy celebration; Dunsford records the occasion, and so does Wesley.

From the journal of John Wesley—

"There was a sermon preached at the Old Church before the

Trustees of the School, At half an hour past twelve the morning service began, but such insufferable noise and confusion I never saw before in a place of worship—no, not even in a Jewish Synagogue. The clergy set the example, talking and laughing during the greater part of the prayers and sermon . . ."

From the pen of Dunsford—

"In the month of September, this year, a great number of gentlemen's servants whose Masters were then in Tiverton, at the annual meeting of Blundell's Grammar School, where many of them had been educated, having procured a fife and drum, and a mob to attend them, came upon John Wesley, when preaching amid a large congregation, and interrupted him so much, that he was obliged to desist, and was taken by a gentleman from the tumult to prevent the injuries threatened to his person."

Sadly, reading between the lines, it would seem, amongst so much learning and scholarship in Divinity, not one there seemed on this occasion to recognise the Spirit of the Lord moving across the country.

Phillip Atherton (Master 1757-1775)

The Rev. Atherton, a fellow of Balliol, had been Usher for eleven years and was elected Master on Daddo's resignation. Martin Dunsford records;

"He was eminent in classical learning, and under his care the reputation of the School was greatly raised. He possessed a good understanding, was of a mild temper and benevolent disposition, which secured his general respect."

The phrase "the reputation of the school was greatly raised" is interesting. During Atherton's time the existing School register was begun, though the register of Scholarship and Exhibitions is complete from the foundation of the School, and it is recorded, for example, that, between the years 1770 and 1780, of the 216 boys that entered the School, 77 went to Oxford alone. The average number of scholars at the School during Atherton's time was around the hundred level. One of Atherton's scholars was John Everleigh who, at the age 33, became Provost of Oriel, Oxford, a post he held until his death in 1814. There is a Memorial to him in St. Peter's, Tiverton.

Richard Keats (Master 1775-1797)

Keats was educated at Winchester and Magdalen Colege, Oxford.

One of his old pupils recorded this interesting account of him:

"There was a peculiarity in his manner, which, successful as it eminently was with him, could scarcely be recommended as a pattern for other masters. It required the singular combination of gravity with drollery (which characterised him) to command the most profound respect. At the same time he carried on a constant playfulness of manner, so much so that a more uniformly severe teacher may with difficulty comprehend how each boy in the School stood in awe of a Master who had a sobriquet for almost every one of them, and who watched the opportunity with the instrument of correction (which he carried over his shoulders, composed of a piece of knotted whip-cord at the end of a stick, nick-named by him "Discipline"), to strike the toes of any boy who rested them against the front board under the desk, affecting to be about to chastise some nearer delinquent, so as to throw off his guard the really comtemplated victim."

Keats introduced into the School the writing of lines and the composition of extempore epigrams on a given subject with only about half an hour's notice beforehand. He is, however, best remembered today for the "Keats Medal", a prize medal instituted by approval of the Feoffees in 1777, for composition and speaking. The first two recipients were:

John Matthew—for an Oration in Latin on the Founder.

Bouchier Wm. Wrey—for Speaking.

Between 1780-1782, a pupil named Archibald Elijah Impey seemed to carry all before him. He received four medals, two for speaking, one for verse competition and one for prose competition. He was the son of Sir Elijah Impey the Chief Justice of Bengal and close friend of Warren Hastings. Impey Senior had been educated at Westminster. He had intended his son to attend the same School, but for some reason the young Impey went against his father's wishes, and came to Blundell's instead.

Impey Senior wrote to his son, possibly in late 1780 or early 1781:

"Your Uncle has shewn me a letter you wrote him from Tiverton, by which you inform him of your having gained a medal at your School. Everything that shews you give attention to your improvement will always be a great satisfaction to me . . . Tho' I was disappointed at your not staying at Westminster, you have so far amply made up for it."

By April 1781, Sir Elijah Impey was coming to terms with his son's choice of School:

"You have so far amply made up for it by your subsequent conduct, that I shall ever forget that you acted contrary to my order. As long as you have the resolution to behave well for the future, it is to me a most ample recompense for what is past."

Later on in that letter there is a hint of the high level of Classical scholarship of that time:

"Among the books you say you read, you do not mention Virgil, Horace, Terence or Caesar's Commentaries. Virgil and Horace I wish you to have at your finger end. I prefer them to all the Latin Poets. Terence and Caesar are elegant and correct authors, you should read Tully's Orations for a more defuse and copious style for yourself.

"In Greek, of the books you say you read, Xenophon and Homer—Homer you should know by heart, and the Cyropaedia should be always in your hand. You should dip into Sophocles—he is a most chaste Greek tragedian. Lucian's Dialogues are in good Greek, and would be useful to you."

Then some additional fatherly advice follows.

"But above all, attend to your religion and reading, and have a particular care that you do not permit a thought to take harbour in your mind, which carried into action or divulged, would disgrace a Gentleman! In this the choice of your company will have the greatest influence. What useful knowledge can you acquire from those who know less than yourself! What interest is served by associating with those whose situation in life is beneath your own! Much harm may be got. Your mind may become vibrated by want of novelty, the exercise and emulation, which conversation with those whose knowledge is more than your own will give it, but it will imperceptibly contrast the habits of those with whom you associate, and it is the place you choose yourself you must be, undoubtedly be classed with them. I should be grieviously mistaken if you should think by anything I have said, that I wish you should servilely follow men of rank higher than yourself, merely in pursuit of some interest to be procured by their favour, or that you should avoid men of merit if their station of life is below yours.

"For I would have you carry this manly consciousness about you, that while you behave like a gentleman you have a right to aspire to any friendship, and what you claim for yourself, be your rank ever so high, you cannot in justice deny to every other man of merit. I have preached, I fear, till you are tired; it is my anxiety for your good . . ."

We now seem to live in times when letters such as that are dismissed as priggish, puritan or pompous. Yet to some, the anxious concern of a dutiful father who loves his son enough to put aside the eighteenth century equivalent of television for a while, and give very serious thought to his son, shines through, with precepts that are worth seriously pondering over even today. Young A. E. Impey became a distinguished barrister.

The School wasn't all Virgil and Horace then; there were times for other activities as well, as another of Keats' former pupils wrote later:

". . . At Tiverton the pugilistic art and amusement of wrestling were patronised. Orchard excursions, a fowl or duck now and then unexpectedly killed, baiting a badger or two, getting into the gates, and keeping a few donkeys for equestran exercises on Saturday and Sunday till turned out towards Cullompton Common on Monday morning, were beneath Mr. Keats' notice . . ."

All was not always sweetness and light. In 1787 Keats faced a rebellion, when the wife of Thomas Wood the Usher demanded to see the contents of the pockets of a pupil suspected of smoking in the prayer room. Maybe it was the degree of female interference that was the principle at stake.

Two of Keats' former pupils became distinguished naval captains. Capt. John Colby, R.N., a Torrington boy, served as a Lieutenant to the *Thunderer,* and saw a great deal of action on this famous ship before, during and after Trafalgar. When he returned from sea he was appointed one of the Commanders of the Royal Hospital at Greenwich.

Capt. Richard Gordan Keats, R.N., G.C.B., the son of the Headmaster, also had a distinguished naval career after he left Blundell's. For his cool conduct and gallantry during the English fleet's attack on the French Squadron on 5th Feb. 1806, he was mentioned in despatches by his Admiral, Sir John Duckworth, who said:

"I cannot be silent, without injustice, to the firm and manly support for which I am indebted to Captain Keats, and the effect that the system and good order in which I found the *Superb* must ever produce; and the pre-eminence of British seamen could never be more highly conspicuous than in this contest."

The French fleet were defeated after two hours of fighting; three of the five vessels were captured and the other two retired in great difficulties.

For this Capt. Keats also received the thanks of Parliament and a handsome present of an engraved ceremonial sword of honour from the Lloyds' Patriotic fund.

Interior of Old Blundell's by Rudge

5
The Masters 1800-1850

Rev. William Page Richards, LL.D. (Master 1797-1823)

"It is the privilege of Schoolmasters to lick creation, and it seemed to us that Dr. Richards not merely licked his people, but in doing so beat all rivals out of the field."

(Artemus Ward.)

RICHARDS of this flagellatory memory reigned over Blundell's during that period of history that included Trafalgar and Waterloo. He came to Blundell's from Winchester, and New College Oxford. Contemporary opinions of Richards seem to vary, but he certainly did not go unnoticed. Despite his great academic skills, Richards did not major on the comfort of his pupils. Snell records the following:

"Breakfast consisted of a roll with a small quantity of milk; "tea" was breakfast over again, and supper there was none. At dinner the boys had only one carver—an old woman who used her fingers and knuckles as freely as her carving knife. The meat, too, was sometimes brought on the table portentously 'high'. Morning ablutions were performed at a pump, and the hardihood of the boys was increased still further by the variations of temperature to which they had to submit. During the winter gales it was by no means a rare event for sleet to find its way through the unceiled roof and drop on the boys' copy books, while at other times all writing had to be suspended because the ink in the desks was frozen."

Yet not all the pupils complained, as the following letter of that period would indicate:

(Extract from a letter written home (Wales) by a fourteen-year old boy, new to Blundell's in 1818):

"... There is a little stream near here called the Lowman which overflowed last night and inundated us all. The water was four inches deep in the school-room and hall where we have our meals, and even made its way to Mr. Richards' drawing-room, so there is a little bustle here now. I mention this because it is an old rule of the School that, when the water rises to a certain mark, the boys are to have a holiday as is the case today, otherwise I should not have been able to have written to you till next week . . . You wished to know every particular as to the School. I think it is a very good one, and I trust I shall improve under Mr. Richards' care. Tell Tom and Henry that Latin verse is a very essential requirement here, as I have to do about twenty lines a week (but the class does thirty) in our play hours, and two themes, an English and Latin one every week. I will tell you the books I read that you may satisfy yourself. They are Caesar, Virgil, Horace, Homer. As to Mr. Richards, I still like him very much; he is very careful of the boys if they are unwell, or have colds, or anything the matter with them, so that you have no reason to be anxious on that account. . .

"We have prayers read every night before we go to bed by one of the monitors. We must be tolerably expeditious in getting into bed, because Mr. Richards comes up in about two or three minutes after, and if we are not all into bed, he is very angry. Sometimes the boys hear him come up, perhaps before they have pulled up their trousers and when they try to jump into the bed in that state, they get entangled in them so that there is fine fun sometimes.

"If you send a box I should like to have a neat penknife with two blades that is very sharp, and if you could send a hone to sharpen it upon, and plenty of paper, as there is so much writing in the School that we use full three sheets of this sized paper (quarto) every week, and likewise send some fine paper, a good quantity, for letters, and sealing wax and wafers, as it will be cheaper than having them here .

"If Tom has got any books that he thinks will be useful, he might send them, such as Cornelius, Nepos, Xenophon's *Memorabilia,* or *Cyropaedia.* As to paying the postage of the letters, I think you need not do that, as Mr. Richards pays for them all and not the boys. Don't make yourself uneasy by thinking that I am uncomfortable here, or anything of that kind, for it is not the case."

The writer apparently went from Blundell's School to Oxford, where he had a distinguished career. He took a first class and became Fellow and Tutor of his College, Vinerian Scholar and Proctor.

Richards seems to have introduced to Blundell's a custom from Winchester, the singing outdoors by torchlight of *Dulce Domum*.

"Towards the close of the winter half year, the boys used to subscribe for purchase of tar barrels and torches. A bonfire was lit in the centre of the green—each boy standing round torch in hand, whilst *Dulce Domum* was sung. This was done for two or three nights in the last week of term according to the amount of the funds collected."

(Mahood.)

One Old Blundellian, John J. A. Boase, at Blundell's 1809-1814, records this ceremony as his most pleasant remembrance of Blundell's ". . . and there still rings in my ears *Nunc est tempus ire domum.*"

The episode of Richards flogging Jack Russell has already been discussed earlier. There was another nineteenth century tradition concerning Richards and the lively Russell that was certainly circulated during Russell's lifetime.

"Dr. Richards had some very fine grapes growing against the garden wall, under the boys' bedroom window. 'Jack was as good as his master', and the young scamp was wont to be let down in a clothes-basket by night, by his mates, to the region of the grapes, and to return with a supply when handed up.

"The Doctor noticed how rapidly his grapes disappeared, and learning from his man John the cause, took his place under the vine with his gardener, who was ordered to lay hold of the boy in the basket and muffle his mouth, lest he should cry out. This he did when Russell descended, and Richards took his place in the clothes-basket. The boys hauled away, wondering at the ascension of weight, but when they saw the Doctor's head level with the window, panic stricken, they let hold of the rope and away went Dr. and basket to the bottom."

Several very distinguished men were pupils of Richards. These included Dr. James Amiraux Jeremie, who was Dean of Haileybury, Regius Professor of Divinity at Cambridge 1850-1870, and Dean of Lincoln; Dr. Francis Fulford, first Metropolitan of Canada, and Sir Charles Edward Trevelyan, who reformed the Civil Service, and who was Governor of Madras, and brother-in-law to Lord Macaulay. There was also the distinguished essayist, Abraham Hayward. Hayward always blamed the severe discipline and diet at Blundell's for his permanent ill-health (though he lived to be 82), yet he always spoke well of his old School, calling it "the Eton of the West."

While Colby was serving in the *Thunderer*, a much younger Blundellian, who had left School also served in the Battle of Trafalgar, as A.D.C. to Capt. Israel Pellow, (later Admiral and brother to the other famous Admiral Edward Pellow, Lord Exmouth), of the *Conqueror*. A. R. B. Thomas writes. "The *Conqueror* was the fourth ship of the starboard line, that took the *Buccentaur* as well as assisting in the capture of *Santissima Trinidad* and another French battleship. The *Buccentaur* was the French Admiral Villeneuve's ship. William Hicks describes in a letter home how he took a message from the Captain to the first Lieutenant just before the latter was killed. After the battle the second-in-command of the French fleet was interred in Tiverton Castle along with other French Naval Officers."

In 1873 a former pupil of Richards was to play a major rôle in a Royal Celebration. The now elderly Parson Jack Russell, that veritable Nimrod, then a guest of the Prince of Wales at Sandringham, danced the old year out and the new year in with H.R.H. the Princess of Wales, later to be Queen Alexandra.

Frank Pepper, in his excellent appreciation of Jack Russell emphasises that as well as being an accomplished sportsman, Russell was a very conscientious parson . . .

> "But it must not be supposed that his live of hunting, and of other forms of sport, made him in any way unique. At the time when he came to Swymbridge there were twenty parsons in the Exeter diocese who kept their own packs of hounds, and many more who rode regularly to hounds two or three times of week. What made Russell outstanding among his clerical contemporaries in the hunting field was the amazing stamina and endurance that reinforced his enthusiasm, even in his old age.
>
> "When he was 79, and staying at Ivybridge, he spent the entire week hunting, and left there to ride home at two o'clock on Saturday afternoon. He road the seventy miles to Tordown, arriving at midnight, ate a good supper, slept soundly and rose refreshed to conduct three services in the parish church next day.
>
> "In 1873 the Prince of Wales heard that Russell was staying at Marham Hall in Norfolk and invited him to Sandringham. The Prince so enjoyed Jack's company that he invited him back for Christmas. 'And put a sermon in your pocket', said the Prince, a command which gave Russell the vast pleasure of preaching in Sandringham church.
>
> "On his return the churchwardens called on him with a special

request that on the following Sunday he should 'praych the zame zermon as 'ee prayched to the Purnce and Purncess.'

'Russell promised he would. The news spread through the parish and when Sunday came the church was packed.

"When Russell mounted the pulpit there was a deep silence. Everyone could sense the anticipatory excitement with which the congregation awaited the treat to come.

"The result was an anti-climax.

"At the close of the service one of the wardens followed Russell into the vestry to voice the hurt disappointment of them all.

" 'Us've yerred thicky ole thing a score of times before. Twas the Purnce's zermon thee promised us. That's what they com'd to yer.'

" 'And that's what they got,'' said Russell blandly. 'That was the sermon I preached at Sandringham, and why not? The gospel is the same for prince and peasant.' "

The Bishop of Exeter spoke Parson Jack Russell's epitaph when someone complained to him of Russell as "a man who kept a pack of hounds for forty years in defiance of his ecclesiastical superiors". "If," said the bishop, "all the parishes in my diocese were as well worked as Mr. Russell's has been at Swymbridge I should not have all the anxieties I have now."

Dr. Richards retired in 1823 a wealthy man, having amassed a fortune of £60,000 out of the School, Yet he left a very prosperous School. There were over 100 boarders and over 200 pupils in all.

Rev. Aldersey Dicken D.D. (Master 1823-1834.)

Dr. Dicken was the third old Blundellian to become Headmaster. He was greatly liked and "had the presence of a Bishop". Whilst a pupil at Blundell's he had won the Keats' Medal for both speaking and composition, and had gained an exhibition to Sydney Sussex, Cambridge. A twelfth wrangler he was elected fellow and Tutor of St. Peter's College. He took his Doctor of Divinity in 1831 after he became Headmaster of Blundell's. Dicken was instrumental in introducing mathematics as a regular subject in the School. The lower Master at that time was Dr. Boulton, a martyr to gout. It was Mrs. Boulton who drew those delightful illustrations of Blundell's at the dawn of the Victorian age, and their pretty daughter Antonia was deemed to be one of the greatest attractions of the School, and like Miss Arabella Ashworth in 1975, had a "marked civilising effect on the boys".

It would appear that Dr. Dicken was greatly liked and respected outside the School. A local Devon paper wrote in 1837 of him: "It is acknowledged on all hands that an instructor more amiable or kindhearted, united with such extensive and varied learning and indefatigable research, has never presided over this noble establishment."

A year before Dr. Dicken resigned his post, a boy of 12 entered Blundell's, "a tall big jointed boy, with his long black hair falling over the collar of his jacket"—and very fond of football. His name was Frederick Temple. He was to become Archbishop of Canterbury and have the honour of placing the crown on the head of King Edward VII.

Henry Sanders ('Sas' 1834-1847.)

Blundell's under 'Sas'

"My first sight of the School was all that I could have hoped for. The entrance through the iron gates, with the lodges on each side, revealed the picturesque building at the end of the green surrounded by beautiful lime trees, then lovely in their nakedness, and the causeway parting half-way up led to the two porches, which divided the building into three equal parts. I had heard nothing about the School, but I was to be under the care of the son of an old Indian friend of my Father's, and I was assured that he would make my entrance easy and pleasant. I was not deceived in him, and I owe more to him than I can well speak of. He was in the Monitors—what at other Schools would be the sixth form, and he slept in the two bedded room, and the only one in Sas' house, and I was to share his room. My first evening was pleasant enough. I was shewn where I was to sit in the Hall for meals, and a lock-up assigned to me, the last one on the left hand of the third row. I was delighted with my bedroom. There was a table with one basin and a jug on it, and in another corner a desk with a cupboard over it. My friend drew for me a picture of the room, which I still have.

"The beds were unlike any I have ever seen, or indeed since seen. They were box-beds, and I believe were so constructed that all the bedding could be put into the box, and the bedsteads folded up into it. I do not think that they were ever thus used, but the boys had found a very good use for the boxes. Lights were of course put out at a certain time, and then if a boy wanted to read a book, he would hang his counterpane over the front of the box and light his candle, which was stuck onto a stick fixed into the side of the box. Occasionally 'Sas' (Sanders) would make a round of the bedrooms,

14. The 1882 buildings today from the West. (Michael Huggins).

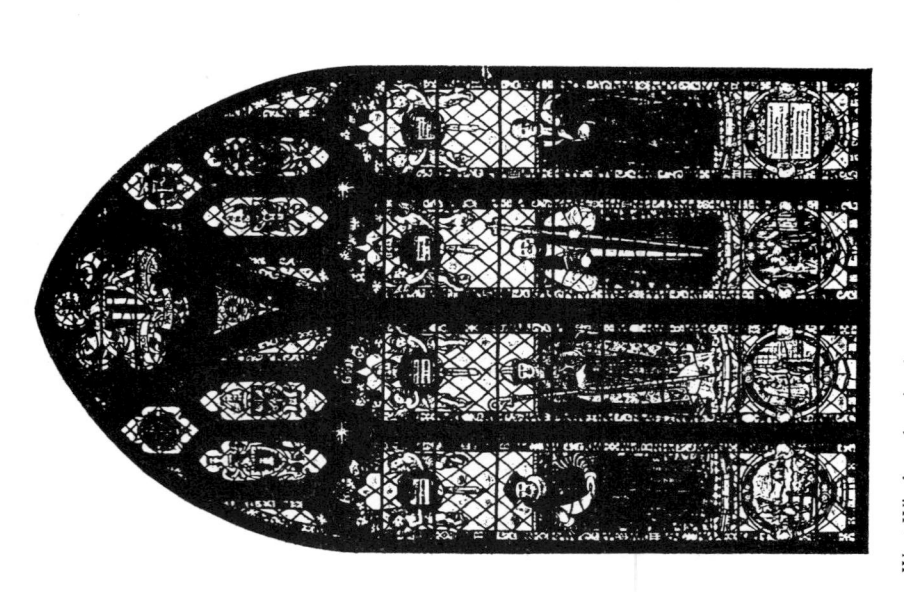

Contrasting stained glass windows, Blundell's School Chapel.

15. West Window showing l. to r. Peter Blundell, Bishop Stapleton, Archbishop Temple, A. L. Francis.

16. Commemorating the girls of Gorton House 1976 in the Chapel Extension.

and catch a boy with a light, and sometimes a boy would go to sleep, and the box and counterpane would catch fire, but it made no difference, and after a short time the practice began again. The next morning we got up at half-past six by candlelight, and went into School at seven. There were three call-overs, at 7, 7.05, and 7.15 a.m. The two first were called by a 'lie-a-bed', with no Master or monitor present; the third was called by a monitor, and at that Sas was present and all the monitors. The monitors took it in turn by weeks to call over, and none of them came into School until 'Sas' entered at 7.15 a.m. Each monitor had a small boy to call over for him at 7.00 and 7.05 a.m., and this boy had the privilege of lying in bed for an extra quarter-of-an-hour on the weeks in which he was off duty, hence his title of 'lie-a-bed'. If a boy failed to answer *adsum,* he was fined 1d., 2d. and 3d. according to his being absent at the first, second and third call-over. The fines were deducted from his *pays* on Saturday, and if he had not sufficient to pay he had *non sol* put after his name, and the fine was taken out by a short and painful process. At nine we went into the Hall for breakfast. I was rather surprised to find that this apparently consisted of a penny roll and a small pat of butter and a bowl of milk. This was in 1846, the last year of the Protection, and a penny roll looked very small indeed for a hungry boy who had been at work for two hours. However, I found that this was not to be all my breakfast. I was invited to join a party of three other boys, who drank together, and I had a capital breakfast of coffee, fried bacon and potatoes, besides my minute pat of butter. One boy out of each set was allowed by the monitors, who kept order, to go into the kitchen, where he could make tea, coffee or cocoa, and do various jobs of cooking, but the principal dish of fried bacon and potatoes was procured from Mrs. Folland, Cop's wife, (The Porter was always called Cop for wearing copper boots in time of floods) who lived at the lodge and was a first rate cook. She dressed anything we could afford to get for breakfast, but nothing in my recollection was ever so good as the fried potatoes, and never since have I tasted that dish in such perfection. At ten we went into School again, and had a good dinner at one, then two hours School in the afternoon, and supper at six. This was as primitive as breakfast, and consisted of bread, cheese and a mug of beer, but the drinking parties were allowed to have what they liked to get, at their own cost, as at breakfast.

"I was much impressed with the interior of the School. It was a long room with an open roof, lighted by mullioned windows. It was divided into upper and lower School by a passage running through the middle of it to the porch, and over the passage was a gallery leading to a room over the porch. The walls were wainscotted up to the sills of the windows, and two rows of seats or blocks, one higher than the other, ran round the room. These were divided into three sets for six classes, monitors, third form, upper and lower second, and upper and lower first. I was put into the upper second, and the next half year into the third form. All the woodwork of the roof and blocks were extremely massive, and it was a tradition that all the wood was Spanish chestnut taken from the wrecks of the Armada, just as the ponies on Exmoor were sprung from Arab horses which were cast ashore from the Armada. (I had for nearly 20 years an Exmoor pony, which had all the points of an Arab, and was as tame and affectionate as any Arab told in story). Not only were the panels covered with the names of former boys, but large pieces had been sawn off the blocks, to be turned into snuff boxes as memorials of the School. All the blocks except those below monitors and third form, had desks in front of them, these two blocks being unused except on the awful occasion of a flogging. Then 'Sas' called out "Bring me a birch!" The junior of the third form left the School, went down to the Porter's lodge, received a birch from the Porter, and brought the birch to 'Sas', having carefully beaten it against the walls to knock off any obnoxious buds, which might be too painful.

It was only once that I beheld this operation, and then I had the misfortune to be the junior of the third form!

In the School work I found that I had much to learn. Wordsworth's Greek Grammar and the Eton Latin Grammar were expected to be known by heart from one end to the other, and as they were both new to me, I had hard work to learn them. Before the first examination I made use of my box bedstead, and spent the whole night in getting up the small print in the Accidence of Wordsworth's Grammar—a task that I never have regretted. My other difficulty was the daily task of Latin Verses, and in this I should never have succeeded but for the help and hints of my friend in Monitors. There were of course books of tags handed down from generation to generation, which 'Sas' must have known by heart, but it was surprising how much ingenuity was called out in originating new ideas. One boy who came at the same time as I did, whom we called the Doctor, would not only write an original copy for himself, but actually four or five original copies for his seniors. He was a genius, and distinguished himself at Oxford, winning the Newdigate with a poem in blank verse—the only one I believe that ever did so. Afterwards he was well known as the writer of brilliant articles in the *Times* and other papers.

One institution, for which I have been grateful, was "spouting". Every Friday three boys from monitors and third form used to stand out in the middle of the School and spout, that is, recite a certain number of lines of English poetry with action. My first piece was Milton's *l'Allegro,* which has still for me the tenderness of a first love. 'Sas'' comment on my performance was "Very well said, but no action." After that I took care to follow Shakespeare's advice to actors. For this custom we were known in the town as "tay kettles" by the boys whom we called "chaws". Mr. Blackmore in his too brief description of Blundell's in *Lorna Doone*, says that we called them 'caddes', but that is not my recollection."

The Old School Crest

6
'A Tiverton School for Tiverton People'

DURING the office of the Rev. Henry Sanders ('Sas'), Headmaster between 1834 and 1847, Blundell's reached a high water mark in its history. The level of scholarship there was very high and Mathematics had already been introduced by Dr. Aldersey Dicken, himself an Old Blundellian. The number of pupils had now reached the 200 level which included 70 boarders in the Headmaster's and Usher's houses combined. The well known essayist Abraham Hayward (1801-1884), translator and editor of *The Law Magazine,* referred frequently to Blundell's as "The Eton of the West", as mentioned previously, for by then generations of the sons of the most famous Devon families had been educated there, as well as many from further afield. Frederick Temple, himself a pupil of 'Sas', in an Old Boys' speech on 16th January 1896, reminiscing on the period of 'Sas', was able to quote a comment made by the then Headmaster of Harrow. "I wish, Mr. Sanders, I had as fine a School as you have got".

However, in 1847 a disaster struck the School that almost resulted in its closing down. There had been from time to time controversy between the town of Tiverton and the School. The first mention of it seems to have been on 19th June 1695, when the Feoffees, after agreeing to "demand performance of ye covenant of ye Mayor under the common Seale for repaving of the highway before the School wall and gate", went on to deal with something much more serious "and also demand of ye ten householders most in ye subsidy booke of His Majesty to admit all the children of forreiners now in ye said School according to Mr. Peter Blundell's will, and if they shall refuse them our Treasurer to proceed in Lawe in our names as he shall be advised."

One hundred and thirty years later the matter between Town and School came to a serious head, mainly through the rough treatment that the day boys received at the hands of the boarders, best described by Blackmore in *Lorna Doone,* for Blackmore was probably writing an account of what actually happened in his own day at Blundell's.

". . . We came out of School at 5 o'clock, as the rule is upon Tuesdays. According to custom, we drove the day boys in brave rout, down the Causeway from the School porch even to the gate where Cop has his dwelling and duty. Little it recked us and helped them less, that they were our founders citizens, and haply his grandnephews (for he left no direct descendants), neither did we much enquire what their lineage was. For it had long been fixed among us, who were of the house and chambers, that these same day boys were all "caddes", as we had discovered to call it, because they paid no groat for their schooling, and brought their own commons with them. In consumption of these, we would help them, for our fare in hall fed appetite, and while we ate their victuals we allowed them freely to talk to us. Nevertheless we could not feel, when all the victuals were gone, but that these boys required kicking from the premises of Blundell's. And some of them were shopkeepers' sons, young grocers, fell mongers, and poulterers, and these to their credit, seemed to know how righteous it was to kick them. But others were of high family, as any need be in Devon, Carews and Bouchiers, and Bastards, and some of them would turn round sometimes, and strike the boy that kicked them. But to do them justice, even these knew they must be kicked for not paying."

One might sympathise with these townsfolk for objecting to being treated as inferiors, and with their newly found urban rights following the Reform Act of 1832 and the Municipal Reform Bill of 1835, they openly aired their grievances over the School through protest meetings held in the town. They did not just protest about bullying, but desired to introduce fresh subjects into the School and wished to have more local say in the handling of the Trustees' money. What could have remained a local matter that might have been settled possibly with a bit of give and take on both sides got overheated and out of hand. Legal proceedings were instigated against the School by the Town because of the boarders. The town was led by their local M.P., John Heathcote (1783-1861). Heathcote, who was the largest employer of labour in the town, was not a Devon man himself. Born in Duffield, Derbyshire, his mechanical inventions in lace making, textiles, and the spinning trade had produced a fresh boom for the town of Tiverton when he moved there after the Luddites had destroyed his machinery in Loughborough. Heathcote had set his heart on social reform and took up the townspeoples' cause against Blundell's through a long legal battle. He appointed as Barrister Richard Bethell (later Lord Westbury, 1800-1873), a man with a blistering tongue who later was to wage a remorseless war against the clergy in general and Bishops in particular after the *Essays and Reviews Controversies*. Mahood quotes the *Dictionary of National Biography* which observes that he (Bethell) "exercised an extraordinary influence over the easy mind" of Vice Chancellor Sir Lancelot Shadwell. Nash in his *Life of Lord Westbury* quotes a legal wit of the day: "Why is Shadwell like King Jeroboam? Because he had set up an idol in Bethel". (1 Kings XII. 28-30). Shadwell was also influenced in his ruling by the case the Manchester citizens had against Manchester Grammar School, though it was rather a different case from the one between the Town and the Trustees of Blundell's. On 29th October 1846, the Vice Chancellor of England delivered his verdict:

"Neither the Master or Usher ought to receive any payments from or in respect of the boys educated in the said School, or ought to take any boarders; and that none but boys educated as free scholars *vide voce,* scholars free of expense in the said School, according to the direction of the said Will, as varied by the decree, ought to be eligible to the said scholarships and exhibitions . . ."

It would appear on reflection that Peter Blundell had a far greater vision for the School than the nineteenth century townsfolk. He had made a provision of "forreyners":

". . . that in the said School shall not be taught above the number of one hundred and fiftie scolars at any one tyme, and those from tyme to tyme of children born or for the most part before their age of sixe yeares brought upp in the Towne or Parrish of Tyverton aforesaid And if the same Number be not filled upp my Will is that the wante shall be supplyed with the Children of Forreyners and those Forreyners only to be received and admitted from Tyme to Tyme forever with the assent and allowance of such tenne householders of the said Towne of Tyverton aforesaid as for the tyme beinge shall be most in the subsidie Bookes of our Sovereigne Lady the Queen as Majesty and her successors for ever and not otherwise And my blessing and desier is that they from tyme to tyme will make choice of the Children of such Forreyners as are of honest Reputation and feare God without regarding the riche above or more than the poore . . ."

Benjamin Incledon comments (1804) on this. "The schools will contain many more than 150 boys but it does not appear that there ever was that number educated in them at one time. For half a century past, from my own memory, I can declare, the number has not at any time much exceeded 100. At present there are only 96; so that it seems unnecessary to make a Distinction between Natives and Forreigners . . ."

Had not Samuel Butler (Master, 1604-1647), under the gimlet eye of Popham, brought scholars to board with him?

Sanders immediately resigned. The School Trustees were faced with bearing the vast cost of litigation, estimated at about £11,000, so certain endowments had to be sold—all this at a time when New Schools like Wellington, Clifton, Cheltenham and Marlborough had either been recently founded or were in the process of foundation. When the Rev. John Bickley Hughes, who had been second Master under Sanders, re-opened the School in 1847, only 17 boys from the Town turned up (though there were 30 boys on the roll).

There seems here to be a very sharp and clear lesson for the age in which we now live, an age when people often get political bees in their proverbial bonnets and set their energies on the abolition of this institution or that custom by highlighting certain failings—many such failings, which, as in the case of Blundell's, could be easily redressed (possibly by a firm word from the Headmaster). Schools such as Blundell's were founded by great men with great vision. One could wonder what is the real vision of these 20th century Luddites save that of abolition. Unless abolition is accompanied by replacement with something far greater, the vision is very small indeed. The job of demolition is not generally regarded as such a skilled craft as that of building. What had been carefully built up over 250 years was almost destroyed overnight, and Blundell's was very nearly reduced almost to the status of a small town Grammar School.

> One pupil of that period recalled in later years the sad occasion. "After my third half-year Mr. Heathcote's lawsuit against the Trustees was won by the cleverist of Lawyers, Richard Bethell, and the boarders were turned adrift. The books in the School library were divided among us, and I still have mine, which are sacred in my eyes. The School was a rough one, but we all loved it and there was real grief in the hearts of all of us, and tears in some eyes, when we said goodbye to 'Sas' and passed through the gateway for the last time."

The *Fortnightly Review* of 1884 in an article devoted to the life of Abraham Hayward, Q.C., seemed to hint at the loss caused in 1847 by stating that Hayward "was educated at Blundell's School, at Tiverton", then adding these words: "then a West Country Winchester". In recalling the case many years later, the *Blundellian* of May, 1953 summed up this unfortunate chapter in the School history as follows: "We are left to wonder at the muddled idealism of those who pleaded for disaster, at the blindness of the judge who conceded it, and the courage and devotion of those who inherited, circumvented and finally overcame it."

The Interior of Old Blundell's — *Rudge*.

7
Blackmore and Temple

Two of Blundell's most famous men were educated under 'Sas'. The first was Richard Dodderidge Blackmore and the second was Frederick Temple.

R. D. Blackmore

Richard Dodderidge Blackmore, M.A. was born in 1825. He was educated at Blundell's, as were his father and grandfather before him, and Exeter College, Oxford. Although called to the Bar at the Middle Temple in 1852, this tall thick-set man spent most of his life market gardening and also writing poetry and novels, which as a farmer would claim today, helped cover his losses; though to his credit, Blackmore cultivated no less than 600 varieties of pears. To most people the name R. D. Blackmore is linked with what has been described as a work of singular charm, vigour and imagination, *Lorna Doone*. This romance of Exmoor recalls 'the savage deeds of the outlaw Doones in the depth of Bagworthy Forest, the beauty of the hapless maid brought up in the midst of them, the plain John Ridd's Herculean power, and . . . the exploits of Tom Faggus.' In writing *Lorna Doone*, Blackmore did for the West Country what Scott did for the Highlands and Hardy for Wessex. There have been American films of *Lorna Doone,* there have been English films, there has been a television series; that excellent childrens magazine *Look and Learn* started a picture serialisation of it in May 1981 (beautifully drawn, yet old Blundell's so graphically incorrect that poor Peter Blundell and Sir John Popham must have turned in their graves). All this we would hope would stimulate youngsters and adults alike to sit down and read the actual book from cover to cover, complete and unabridged, for that is the only way to capture *Lorna Doone*. Yet *Lorna Doone* was not Blackmore's favourite work, he preferred, *The Maid of Sker* and *Springhaven,* though Girt Jan Ridd was his favourite character. To some old Blundellians there is another work of his that is very special;

it is found in the *Oxford Book of English Verse,* a moving work that gives a clue to the strength that lay within the man.

Dominus Illuminatio Mea

In the hour of death, after this life's whim,
When the heart beats low, and the eyes grow dim,
And pain has exhausted every limb—
The lover of the Lord shall trust in Him.

When the will has forgotten the lifelong aim,
And the mind can only disgrace the frame,
And a man is uncertain of his own name—
The power of the Lord shall fill this frame.

When the last sigh is heaved, and the last tear shed,
And the coffin is waiting beside the bed,
And the widow and child forsake the dead—
The angel of the Lord shall lift this head.

For even the purest delight may pall,
And power must fail, and pride must fall,
And the love of the dearest friends grow small—
But the Glory of the Lord is all in all.

The poet, Sir John Squire, himself an old Blundellian, stated in the Blackmore Centenary address, 12th June 1925, "if you forget his other nineteen books, his translation from Virgil and *Lorna Doone,* and if he had never produced anything but this poem, the school could be proud of having had a man who wrote such perfect literature."

Blackmore died on 20th January 1900, the same day as John Ruskin.

As visitors leave the Cathedral Church of St. Peter, Exeter, they cannot help but notice the memorial to R. D. Blackmore.

Frederick Temple
"He was a good man and he did good things". (Alicia C. Percival, *Very Superior Men)*

Although today Blackmore is probably the most famous of Saunder's pupils, Frederick Temple was undoubtably the greatest; not because of his brilliance or because he was eventually to become Archbishop of Canterbury, but because of his strength of character, his clarity of vision, his ability for sheer hard work, his downright guts and determination in times of adversity and unpopularity, and his ability to accept leadership without abdicating responsibility.

Born in the Ionian Islands in 1821, Temple gained the Balliol Scholarship from Blundell's in 1838. These were the days when a thorough knowledge of Latin and Greek grammar was required, and a great stress was laid on verse composition and recitation in Latin and English. The authors read for that year were Thucydides, Plautus, Demosthenes, Sophocles, Virgil, Herodotus, Cicero, Homer, Horace and Lucretius. The boys were also encouraged by rewards to commit passages of the classics to memory, and time was left for private reading. In the Headmaster's mark book for 1838 are notes of the proficiency of the upper boys, not only in Euclid and Algebra, but also in Trigonometry and conic sections. Temple recorded once that Dr. Jenkins, the then Master of Balliol, was prejudiced against Blundell's men because they entered Balliol through a closed scholarship. His initial encounter with Temple was blunt, "You Blundell's Scholars have certainly a great advantage", he said haughtily to Temple, "coming up as you do, very inferior men into a society of very superior men; some of you are improved by it and some are not". Yet he soon conceded that Temple was made of different mettle from what he had presumed, and later his attitude towards Temple changed to that of kindness and generosity. Temple eventually gained two First Classes. General Sir George Chesney recalled the occasion in later years during an O.B. Speech in 1893. He said that, when a new boy at Blundell's in 1838, he was told that there was to be a whole holiday the following day because Temple had taken a Double First. Chesney admitted that at that time he had no idea what taking a Double First meant but as a lad he had keen conception of what a whole holiday meant.

Temple is best remembered as a great cleric, yet he was also a man who had revolutionary ideas on education which quite startled many of his contemporaries. After a few years as Fellow of Balliol and lecturer in Mathematics and Logic, during which period he was ordained by Bishop Wilberforce of Oxford, Temple became Headmaster of Kneller Hall, which was an unsuccessful scheme involved in the training of masters for workhouses and penal schools. Temple recommended that the project be dropped. Meanwhile his able writing had reached the admiration of the Prince Consort so that in 1856 Temple was appointed Chaplain Ordinaire to the Queen. In 1858 he succeeded Tait as Headmaster of Rugby, a school which benefitted greatly from Temple's vision and drive. Arthur Stanley, Dean of Westminster, himself educated at Rugby under Arnold, regarded Temple as the best Headmaster in England and

Matthew Arnold said that "Temple resembled more than any other man I have known . . . my late father". At Rugby, Temple built a Science Laboratory and instilled there a fresh concept, that of Scholarships in Natural Science. It was now 35 years since William Webb Ellis . . . "with fine disregard for the value of football as played in his time, first took the ball in his arms, and ran with it, thus originating the distinctive features of the Rugby game." Yet Temple, although aware that strong games traditions had developed through this, boldly did much to reform the games at this school. Temple was also able to skilfully steer Rugby away from a crisis similar to that which had nearly destroyed his old school a few years earlier. The situation was similar. The townsfolk of Rugby were up in arms because they believed that they were being deprived by the non-local character of the school. Temple was well aware of the formidable damage that had been done to Blundell's in the Heathcote dispute, and was determined to save Rugby from a similar fate. This he succeeded in doing by proposing, in his usual particularly careful detail, that a second school be formed out of the Lawrence Sherrif foundation funds to be especially geared to the requirements of the town.

It was during his time at Rugby that Temple faced a heavy storm of criticism and censure by the Church because of his involvement in H. B. Wilson's publication *Essay and Reviews* in 1860. Temple wrote the first chapter, choosing as his subject *The Education of the World*. It seems that it was not actually what Temple wrote that caused this storm, but his implied association in doing so with the writings of Wilson, Jowett, Williams, and Goodwin, some of the other essayists. Wilson for example, seemed to introduce a form of theological Danegeld in his essay on the *National Church,* whilst Goodwin was obviously influenced by the writings of Lyell, Chambers, Wallace, and Darwin in his essay on the *Mosaic Cosmogeny.* His critics demanded that he, Temple, disassociate himself from the others and withdraw his essay. Temple refused, for the terms of reference had been made clear to him before he wrote his essay, being that each contributor would present his own views, and that they were not out to present a united front, nor were they expected to agree with the views of the other contributors. Instead he later published his own Rugby Sermons which clearly demonstrated that his own beliefs were not as his opponenets suspected. One Rugby schoolboy was able to reassure his worried mother: "Dear Mother, Temple's alright, but if he turns Mahometan, all the School will turn too". Still, led by Bishop Samuel Wilberforce, almost the whole weight of the House of Bishops were against the essays, including Bishop Tait, Temple's friend and predecessor at Rugby. The contributors Williams and Wilson were within the jurisdiction of the Court of Arches and were convicted of heresy. This decision was later quashed by Bethel, now Lord Westbury, after an appeal to the Judicial Committee of the Privy Council.

"Dear Mother, Temple's alright, but if he turns Mahometan, all the School will turn too."

When Gladstone appointed Temple to the See of Exeter, a fresh storm of opposition arose, led this time by Lord Shaftesbury. Edward Pusey, leader of the Oxford Movement, stated that the choice of Temple was "the most frightful enormity ever perpetrated by a Prime Minister", and one bishop wrote to *The Times* stating that Temple's appointment was "a blow from which the Church of England might rally for a time, but afterwards could never be the same", but Gladstone remained adamant. Only a quorum of three bishops were willing to take part in Temple's consecration. Nonetheless Temple proved his opponents were mistaken, not by lengthy debate of pleading his cause, but by the extremely capable way in which he undertook all his pastoral duties. He was very hardworking and still maintained his interest in education. Doris M. Bradbeer, in her book on the Exeter Grammar Schools, *Joyful Schooldays,* pays tribute to Temple for his part in revitalising the education of that city:

". . . This was largely the work of Frederick Temple, then Bishop of Exeter, who was a member of the Commission, and brought into being the two Secondary Schools of Maynard and Bishop Blackall (both girls schools), thus establishing a complete system of secondary education in the City. . . .

". . . Dr. Temple set out the principles on which he based his proposals in a letter to the Mayor on 5th February 1872. In it he pleaded eloquently for the adoption of his scheme for the re-organisation and stressed the desirability of a higher education for girls:- . . . 'No argument is needed to shew how sorely Exeter suffers from the want of a good Grammar School for boys and a good upper School for girls. The wealthier can, of course, provide for themselves. They can send both sons and daughters to a distance, but the great body of the middle class, who will be now for the first time rated, and perhaps heavily rated, for Elementary Schools, have no really efficient Schools for their own children. And although it seems to be thought that there is something especially incongruous in providing an Upper School for girls, I cannot see how it is to be maintained that the middle classes, from the shopkeepers upwards, do not need efficient schooling for their girls as well as for their boys, nor how provision for it is inconsistent with the purpose of a Foundation which aims at the good of the citizens generally. Our ancestors, to whom we owe this Foundation, were wise men. They gave their upper education the completeness, and to their lower the form, that suited their day. We must do the same, or else though we may mimic their acts, we shall not copy the example of their wisdom. . .'

"In the same letter Temple also stressed the right of all sections of the community to a state-aided education, the advantage of home life as opposed to an institutional one, and the degrading affect of charity when it depended on personal favours. He advocated within the city three grades of schools above the elementary."

In 1884 Temple was invited to give the Bampton lectures at Oxford. He chose as his subject, *The Relations between Religion and Science*. In 1885, Temple, a Balliol man, was elected to be honourary fellow of Exeter College, Oxford, and in 1886 he was transferred to the See of London. This time it was a happy and welcome appointment, the calibre of Temple was becoming apparent to all. Again, in London, he worked extremely hard, often up to fourteen hours a day, and he expected hard work and hard study from his sometimes reluctant ordinands. A. L. Francis wrote of Temple, ". . . He could not suffer fools gladly, and had an unerring scent for humbug, pretence, claptrap, or special pleading. To the ambitious cleric who was anxious to undertake the charge of two adjoining parishes on the grounds that they were only two miles apart as the crow flies, Temple replied, 'You're not a crow, you can't fly and you shan't have it.' "

It was remarked of Temple that working men saw in him a friend with whom they could identify. This is best appreciated if one recalls Temple's boyhood. His father, Major Octavius Temple, Lt. Governor of Sierra Leone, died when Temple was only thirteen, leaving the family in circumstances that required hard work and very careful budgeting. As Temple once wrote:

"Although I had an excellent education, I had experience, nevertheless, of a great deal of privation during that time. I knew what it was, for instance, to be unable to afford a fire on cold days and nights, and I knew what it was sometimes to live on very poor fare; I knew what it was—and I think it was the thing that pinched me most—to wear patched clothes and patched shoes. When I mention these things, I do it in order to make you understand how heartily my sympathies go with working men. I believe there is probably at this moment not another man in England who could thrash better than I could. Threshing is gone out of fashion, it is all done by machinery now and there are very few people who learn to thresh. I learnt to plough, and I could plough as straight as any man in the Parish."

Temple's practical concern for the poor was also recorded in the letter he wrote to the Mayor of Exeter:

". . . In our private charities we cannot help aiding the poor as poor; but then we are able, if we so choose, to do it without attaching to our aid any public stamp of poverty, and to take off much of the evil of teaching the lesson of dependence by making the receiver feel that our gift is one of sympathy between man and man, and not a favour between rich and poor. . . .*And even then, the many mistakes we make compel us to feel that our Lord has given us no harder problem to solve than how to aid the poor without doing them harm.* But in dealing with public and permanent institutions, where it is possible to calculate beforehand how aid is to be obtained, it is of priceless importance to give aid in a form that shall encourage self respect and self-reliance. . . .''

Temple succeeded Archbishop Benson to Canterbury in 1896. It was a brief but full primacy that included both the Diamond Jubilee of Queen Victoria and the Coronation of Edward the Seventh. Although now aged seventy-five, his mind remained resolute, astute and clear. He was able during office, along with the Archbishop of York, to firmly grasp some very difficult nettles. For example in 1899 the two Archbishops issued a very able reply to the Pope's encyclical that denied the validity of Anglican orders. In 1900 the two Archbishops gave a very firm ruling against the growing practice of reserving the elements and the use of incense. Temple also spoke strongly against the divisions that were weakening the Anglican Church. In the Jubilee during what would have been a gap in the ceremony, the Archbishop, completely unrehearsed, called for three cheers for Her Majesty, in what the Archbishop of Armagh referred to as "that great hammerstroke of a voice." At eighty, people were concerned as to whether he could stick the two hour pageant of the coming Coronation, yet he did.

"He had known poverty and almost rags; in his education he had to count the cost of candles and fires, yet here he was the chief figure, except the Sovereign, in the most brilliant assembly of our times, the man who the nation by it's chosen representatives had elected to set the Crown upon the head of it's King."

Temple died in harness. He had preached in Canterbury Cathedral on his eighty first birthday, but collapsed whilst speaking for Balfour's Education Bill in the House of Lords, recovering enough to finish most of his speech, except a kindly message for his non-conformist fellow Christians, which, despite his weakening condition, he sent to them the following day. He died three weeks later at Lambeth Palace, a great Christian and a great Victorian, It was written of him: "He rose to

Drawings of Big School and the Library, between the Wars, by Margaret Holman.

17. The Big School.

18. The Library.

19. & 20.   Comparative drawings from Big Field before and after Chapel Extension.

eminence from obscurity, not, as many have risen, by using each step in his preferment as a foothold from which to grasp at a higher place, but by concentrating his many gifts and wonderful energy upon the task he had in hand. . . ."

A. L. Francis made this interesting observation on Temple as a preacher of the Word:

"One striking peculiarity of the Archbishop as a preacher, unless the writer is mistaken, was the sparing use he made of quotations, except from the Bible. The King's message must be delivered straight from heart to heart, and he deliberately put aside all phrases, however splendid, all thoughts, however sublime, which might introduce another personality between himself and those whom he was commissioned to admonish. What his sermons lost in variety and elegance, they gained in authority. . . ."

"As long as I live, wherever I go, if I meet a Blundell's Schoolfellow—whether one with whom I was at School, or one who came in earlier or later times—I shall always consider that our hearts have been brought together by love for the same old School."
Archbishop Frederick Temple.

IMMORTALISED IN BLACKMORE'S "LORNA DOONE" BLUNDELL'S "OLD SCHOOL" AN IMPORTANT EXAMPLE OF AN EARLY SEVENTEENTH-CENTURY GRAMMAR SCHOOL, WHICH HAS BEEN GIVEN TO THE NATIONAL TRUST ON THESE LAWNS JOHN RIDD FOUGHT HIS SCHOOLBOY BATTLE.

The Illustrated London News Picture Library

8

Rev. John Bickley\Hughes (Headmaster 1847-1873)

THERE was a story circulated once that during the time of 'Sas', there was an Undermaster, who although having the correct academic qualifications, was felt by the Trustees to be really lacking in the necessary brilliance and know-how to be teaching at Blundell's. The Trustees decided, apparently, that the best and kindest way to remove him was to write him such a glowing testimonial that he would be able to apply for vacancies for the post of Headmaster in any good School, suggesting in this testimonial that his talents were wasted on anything less. This scheme, however, backfired on them by the sudden resignation of Sanders; for, seeing the vacancy at Blundell's, Hughes, who appears to have been that Master, presented his glowing testimonial as his reference for the now vacant post. The now highly embarrassed Trustees, and probably highly shaken ones after the lawsuit results, had no alternative but to accept his application—with the seeming collapse of the School, probably few good men really wanted the job in any case. Yet, even if this were true, history proved that Hughes was really the very man they needed to guide the School out of that great crisis. His subsequent actions showed that Hughes was probably well aware of his own personal limitations. By acknowledging areas of weakness, Hughes was able to seek the right remedies by bringing into the School first class teachers.

Hughes' nickname "Daddy Hughes" may have been given because he was the patriarch of rather a large family. Having taught at Blundell's during its moments of greatness, he never seemed to entertain any thought of Blundell's reverting to just a town School. The Vice Chancellor of England had spelt out the rules in strict legal terms and made them abundantly clear to the School and apparently restrictive. Hughes set out at first to make the School as attractive educationally as he could by including, as well as the normal grammar subjects of Latin and Greek, Mathematics and Modern Languages, and he also brought in an extra Master who specialised in writing and arithmetic. The new Masters included the Rev. Robert Duckworth, the Rev. D. S. Ingram, later Headmaster of Felsted, and William Folland. The appointment of Duckworth, especially, was a master-stroke. Duckworth, a Cambridge wrangler, was a brilliant mathematician as well as an excellent teacher of the subject. As news got around of Duckworth's appointment, Hughes was flooded by eager enquiries from parents seeking places in the School.

"Neither the Master or Usher . . . ought to take any boarders . . ." said the Vice Chancellor of England. But there were now other Masters who did not live on the Foundation who were neither Headmaster nor Usher. The Chancellor had omitted to mention them, so Hughes encouraged these masters to take boarders, at first a few each, as in the case of Parson Pole and William Folland. Then Hughes made a bolder move still; he persuaded Duckworth and Ingram to open up boarding establishments in the town for the boys. Duckworth initially opened one up at Twyford Place in 1853, but within five years needed to move to a larger establishment in Bampton Street, where he had 50 or more boys at a time.

One of these boys in later years recalled the atmosphere:

". . . As a teacher of mathematics, Mr. Duckworth was unsurpassed. . . . Of his work as a Clergyman in charge of boys, it may be said that he fully realised the weightiness of his charge and did his best to make us good Christians and good Churchmen. The (then) lack of a School Chapel he endeavoured to make up for by reading on Sunday evenings Dr. Vaughan's sermons to the Harrow boys. His favourite discourse was one on the evil of excuses.

"I can see him now shaking with laughter as he listened to a then popular song *The Galloping Snob of Rotten Row* sung by a boy sitting astride a big drum for a steed, which he whacked and thumped as he sang.

"The scholarships gained by his pupils amounted to over £10,000, his most successful pupil being Mr. J. S. Yeo who was second wrangler in the year 1881; but it may be doubted if any School of this size ever obtained a larger number of mathematical scholarships."

These recovery years were tough times, and indeed there seemed to be moments when the Masters wondered if the School would ever make it. Yet they struggled on, sometimes foregoing their salaries, sometimes forking out of their own pockets to finance a promising boy's scholarship, such was their dedication. Tiverton did not oppose Hughes' moves; if the truth were known, certain factions even encouraged him, for the town's victory in 1847 had resulted in loss of trade that hit the pockets of many of the town's shopkeepers and hoteliers. In 1865 a new Government scheme was devised that circumvented the Vice Chancellor's ruling concerning only Free Scholars being eligible for the School's closed Scholarships.

During this period of history the British Empire was rapidly expanding, so gradually more and more former Blundellians turned to the Services and overseas Civil Services for their careers. Typical of such were two brothers, sons and grandsons of Blundellians, Lewis and Henry Wells. Lewis died of yellow fever whilst still a young lieutenant, yet had already taken part in several historic naval encounters, been mentioned several times in despatches and decorated for bravery. He was on his way to take up his appointment as Lieutenant on the Royal Yacht "Victoria and Albert" when he died. Both Lord Wolseley and Sir Henry Brackensbury mention this young officer in their writings, the latter in these terms: "By his death one of the finest, handsomest and bravest officers that ever lived was thus lost to Her Majesty's Navy."

Henry Wells, Lewis' brother, chose the Army, where he was soon recommended for conspicuous gallantry and bravery by General Sir Douglas Stewart. Wells saw remarkable service on the Afghan frontier, India and Persia, and was presented with ceremonial gifts by two successive Shahs of Persia. He died in 1898 when he was 50, still in his prime. Lord Curzon, then Viceroy of India, wrote of him "a gallant, chivalrous, and fearless Englishman, with the honour of the country and his own duty ever before his eyes."

Another distinguished pupil of Hughes who died still young was Thomas Uttermare Cross, who returned to his old School to teach; more of him later.

9

Augustus Lawrence Francis, M.A. (Headmaster 1874-1916)

IN retrospect today it would seem as if J. B. Hughes had paved the way for a man who was to be regarded by many as Blundell's greatest Headmaster, a man who was to guide Blundell's through some very exciting and difficult decisions. A. L. Francis was the son of Judge H. R. Francis. He was educated at Christ's Hospital and Jesus College, Cambridge. He was stroke for the College boat and obtained a first class honours degree in Classics. He taught for a while at Dulwich College before he was appointed, at the age of 26, Headmaster of Blundell's, which makes him one of the youngest Headmasters ever of a major Public School. That particular honour, according to the "Guinness Book of Records", goes to Henry Montague Butler (born 2nd July, 1833), who was appointed Headmaster of Harrow on 16th November, 1859, when aged 26 years 137 days. Butler's first term of office began in January 1860. Francis could possibly have beaten Butler's record if he were to have accepted one of the two offers he received prior to Blundell's at the age of 23. Such was the quality of the man that, no sooner was he settled in Blundell's, than other Schools tried to lure him away. Francis was the first Headmaster of Blundell's who was not in Holy Orders. It was said that for sheer brilliancy of intellect he was unequalled. As a distinguished Latin Scholar he was the joint author of *The Advanced Latin Syntax* and *The English Translation of Martial's Epigrams*. His detailed knowledge of the poet Horace was instrumental in the changing of the School Motto. Up to that time the School Motto had been:-

IN PATRIAM POPULUMQUE FLUXIT
This is shewn clearly in the die of the 1777 Keats medal.

(It is interesting to note here that an earlier problem is still with us if we look at the medal, for on the reverse side the goddess Minerva (or is she a prototype Britannia?) appears once more. Dressed in an early design of corps uniforn, and armed to the teeth, she has seemingly taken up residence, and is busy handing out laurels to a pupil most unsuitably clad.)

Francis remembered that the identical Latin to that used in the ancient motto occurred in *The Odes of Horace,* book three:

fecunda culpae saecula nuptias
primum inquinavere et genus et domos;
hoc fonte derivata clades
In Patriam Poplumque Fluxit.

motus doceri gaudet Ionicos
matura virgo et fingitur artibus
iam nunc et incestos amores
de tenero meditatur ungui;

mox iuniores quaerit adulteros
inter mariti vina, neque eligit
cui donet impermissa raptim
gaudia luminibus remotis,

sed iussa coram non sine conscio
surgit marito, seu vocat institor
seu navis Hispanae magister,
dedecorum pretiosus emptor. etc.

Without attempting to translate for those Philistines who avoided Latin, or those who strove no further than *Puella Nautam Amat* (an early Latin version of *Bobby Shafto),* it is enough to say that for Horace it was not *learning* that flowed out among the people and the country, and the activities of loose women were also lamented.

The motto of Blundell's School was changed to the present motto:-

'PRO PATRIA POPULOQUE'

Having sorted out the problem of the School Motto, Francis was able to turn his attention to the needs of the Royal Commission, and by a slight alteration to a well-known line of Horace, was able to suggest a suitable motto for them in 'Punch' of 20th June, 1906.

"Dulce et decorum est pro patria morari."

Francis was quite happy to vary the mode of communication. For example, in 'Punch' 16th June, 1909, his advice to 'a perplexed Government' was in the vernacular:

"Why shift your ground in hope to save your face?
"The blow will fall in quite another place."

It was while Francis was Headmaster that Blundell's was able to donate this poetical gem to Devonshire—French culture, thereby paving the way for the 'entente cordiale':-

La Foire Du Mont Del.   J. Wyatt

Père Jan, Père Jan, Prête-moi ta jument
Tout le long, sous le long, hors de long dis.
Car je vieux aller à la foire du Mont
Avec Gilbert, Jean Stère, Pierre Greuse, Pierre Davé, André Guidon,
Henri Touton,
le vieux oncle Collé et tous, le vieux oncle Collé et tous.

Et quand reverrai-je ma petite jument?
Tout le long, sous le long, hors de long dis.
Le vendredi ou le samedi, midi,
Avec Gilbert, Jean Stère, Pierre Greuse, Pierre Davé, André Guidon,
Henri Touton,
Le vieux oncle Collé et tous, le vieux oncle Collé et tous.

Vint vendredi, vint samedi, midi,
Tout le long, sous le long, hors de long dis.
Le pauvre père Jan n'a pas sa jument,
Avec Gilbert, Jean Stère, Pierre Gruese, Pierre Dáve, André Guidon,
Henri Touton,
Le vieux oncle Collé et tous, le vieux oncle Collé et tous.

Le vieux père Jan il monte sur le mont
Tout le long, sous le long, hors de long dis.
Il voit sa jument faisant testament,
Avec Gilbert, Jean Stère, Pierre Greuse, Pierre Davé, André Guidon, Henri Touton,
Le vieux oncle Collé et tous, le vieux oncle Collé et tous.

La vielle jument du père elle mourra,
Tout le long, sous le long, hors de long dis.
Le pauvre père Jan sur une pierre il pleura
Avec Gilbert, Jean Stère, Pierre Greuse, Pierre Davé, André Guidon, Henri Touton,
Le vieux oncle Collé et tous, le vieux oncle Collé et tous.

Mais ça ne finit pas l'affreuse affaire,
Tout le long, sous le long, hors de long dis.
Ni, quoiqu'ils soient morts, cette vilaine carrière
Avec Gilbert, Jean Stére, Pierre Greuse, Pierre Davé, André Guidon, Henri Touton,
Le vieux oncle Collé et tous, le vieux oncle Collé et tous.
etc.
Ref. Blundellian March 1894.

This contribution by Blundell's to the study of Linguistics was recorded in an 1881 edition of the Blundellian:- (although presented anonymously, it was actually written by Francis, who had made a particular study of the Devonshire dialect.)

The Devon Verb "To BE"

Present

Singular	*Plural*
Oi be	We'm
Thee beest	Yu'm
'Er be	They'm

Past

Singular	*Plural*
Oi wuz	Us wur
Thee wuz	Yu wur
'Er ave bin	They wur

Future (negative form)
Oi wunt
Thee'd best ways not
Er shanna
Plural regular
Subjunctive mood
Present

Singular	*Plural*
Ef so as oi be	Spoas we'm
Ef so as yu be	Spoas yu'm
Spoas 'er be	Ef so as they'm

Imperfect

Singular	*Plural*
Oi med 'abin	Us moutavbin
(wanting)	Yu moutavbin
Er med 'abin	They moutavbin

Optative or Hortative form

Singular	*Plural*
Oi'd better be	We'm better be
Thee'd better be	Yu'm best ways be
Er'd best be	They'd best moind 'emselves

Imperative

Singular	*Plural*
Yu let oi be (sometimes 'lemme 'lone")	We'm best be
Do'ee now be	Do'ee now be
Lave 'un baide	Lave 'un baide

Verb Infinitive
Present:- Vur tu be
Past:- Tuvabin
Future:- Tu be gwain fur tu be
Gerundive:- Bound fur tu be
Periphrastic Gerundive Conjugation
Oi'm bound for to be
Thee's bound for to be

10

From the Old to the New

*My desire is that these things should be very
well strongly and substantially done."*

Peter Blundell 1599.

    The School Governors and Francis were soon to be making a most difficult but courageous decision on behalf of the School. The School had to move. The initiative was originally made by a far-seeing Tiverton Solicitor and old Blundellian, called William Partridge, and a local surgeon, called Frederick Mackenzie. Like so many Tiverton men they dearly loved Old Blundell's, whose ancient buildings were a great source of pride to them, especially when William Morris, the English poet and artist, who founded the Society for the Protection of Ancient Buildings, wrote very warmly about the early 17th century buildings that had existed apparently untouched with all their fittings, "were neither small nor unimportant, but were beautiful examples of that temperate and peculiar domestic style of architecture which has been a glory to English art". Any suggestion of the School moving from there seems inconceivable, yet these two men also faced up to some very hard facts. Old rivals were expanding, but the town was now built around the four acre site that enclosed the old School. The Endowed Schools Act of 1869 had conferred upon a special Commission very wise and drastic powers for re-organising ancient endowments. The Commission was demanding certain standards and requiring endowed Schools to be graded. An ancient School like Blundell's with its fine endowment and its rich history must remain first class, yet it was becoming apparent that if the School remained in its cramped and old-fashioned condition it would be down-graded. It was not going to be easy to abandon the old building;

but reluctantly the Headmaster and the Governors were persuaded, though other factions held protest meetings to the very end. Even if they moved, would the fine spirit that existed in the old School continue at the new? It was finally decided that despite the financial risks involved, the School must move to a larger and better site. Eventually the Horsdon site, a mile away, was chosen. On 26th January, 1880 the noble Earl of Devon laid the foundation stone, and Dr. Frederick Temple, who was the Bishop of Exeter, led the prayers.

Hayward's of Exeter, who were the Architects, had been told to design a School for 300 boys, but within a modest budget, as the School had never recovered its heavy losses that followed the disastrous litigation forty years earlier. The old Devonian Red Sandstone buildings Hayward designed are unpretentious yet attractive in their simplicity. He took the unusual step of placing the main tower to the north of the facade instead of the traditional centre area. The School moved in May 1882. Eighty eight boys went from the Old School and, with an addition of 12 entries for that term, the total was 100.

Sadly, Duckworth resigned. Possibly he just was not convinced as to the wisdom of the new venture, of, at his age, prepared to sink his own capital into such a risky undertaking. Yet there was a dignity in his departure. "My loyalty to Blundell's will not allow me to make more than general remarks as to the circumstances which led me to sever my connections with it. Cabinet secrets are not to be made public property by those who desert the Cabinet." The School never forgot Duckworth, he had raised the standard of mathematical teaching to a point hitherto unknown; the Duckworth prizes are held in honour of his memory, and his memorial is in St. Peter's Church, Tiverton. In 1884 another great mathematician came to teach at Blundell's—Joseph Midgley Thornton, whose pupils included P. E. Marrack (Senior Wrangler), A. V. Hill (Third Wrangler), and T. Knox Shaw (Fourth Wrangler).

Francis' leadership, enthusiasm and faith in the new venture inspired other master's, and one young master in particular, the Rev. Uttermare 'Tory' Cross, who had himself been educated at Blundell's under Hughes between 1866-1869. Cross did not wait for the new buildings to be completed, but went ahead and sank his own capital into building the first of the new Boarding Houses that surround these buildings today, and completed it even before School House was finished, therefore claiming the right to name it 'The Old House' in happy anticipation of others. Within ten years Westlake, Petergate and North Close had also been built as other masters, totally loyal to Francis' leadership, willingly sank their own capital into the new venture. These houses stand today, large proud buildings, individually very different, reflecting the level of dedication and commitment those late Victorian masters had. Francis House was built later, in 1926, two years after A. L. Francis had died.

After the foundation stone of the New School had been laid, Temple had strongly advocated the building of a Chapel at the new School, recalling the benefit the Chapel at Rugby had been to staff and boys alike. Cross immediately set about canvassing funds for such a School Chapel. The School Chapel Foundation is separate from the School, for the Chapel was built by voluntary subscription, the site being bought from the Governors and placed in the hands of Trustees. It has been built and enlarged entirely by private subscription. All its appointments are gifts, and the oak panelling is a deliberate copy of the panelling that was in Old Blundell's. The Chapel was consecrated in 1883, Cross becoming the first Chaplain to the School, and his infant daughter the first child baptised in the font.

Cross worked on tirelessly for the School, active in the building of the fives courts (later replaced), the swimming pool and the first cricket pavillion. It was he who re-established the *Blundellian*, making the School library responsible for its expenses. To one colleague who thought the magazine would never last and who declared he would eat every number after the third, Cross always sent successive numbers wishing the recipient a good appetite. Yet he died at 41, still young. Francis lost one of his closest friends, and the tribute he gave before the silent School is deep, and very moving.

". . . The lesson, the solemn warning, is written for all to read. Use your strength, as he used it, while you may, as a trust from God in His service, for you cannot tell what day or what hour you may be called upon to surrender your trust and give an account of your stewardship . . ."

To the grief-stricken boys of Old House, Francis, in a gentle kindly way, gave fresh encouragement ". . . As you love the School and as you reverence the memory of the Founder of your House, I beg you to ask yourselves how best under changed conditions you can shew forth that love, that reverence, as action. The best House, the ideal House, the mainstay of the School would not be that which should shew the most Challenge Cups or Prizes won in work or games, but the one whose members—be their numbers great or small—should unite together in hearty, loyal and rational obedience to love and duty, in the fear of God. This were indeed an honourable rivalry and worthy of a great School. . ."

An oak pulpit was erected in 1893 in the Chapel and a spire in 1894 outside, to the memory of Thomas Cross. The spire was later replaced by the existing Chapel tower.

Another Gentleman of that period, who was extremely generous to Blundell's was John Coles. F. I. A. Coles, a farmer's son who was born near Tiverton in 1834, like Peter Blundell of old, rose to high position, though this time in the nineteenth century world of finance, and became a director of the Hudson Bay Company. As a boy he had attended the Chilcott Free School, Tiverton, which had been founded in 1609 by Peter Blundell's nephew and clerk, Robert Chilcott. Though he had never himself been able to go on to Blundell's, Coles keenly recognised the need for such a School, and also the necessity to equip it properly for the coming demand that the twentieth century would place. Amongst other generous gifts, he provided the School with an extremely fine physics Laboratory, possibly one of the first of its kind in such a School. Coles died in 1919 aged 86. The Coles Memorial prizes for Mathematics are named after Coles, who was an actuary. These were exciting days, changes were being made and innovations were on the way. Old habits were not being clung to just for the sake of it. A few years before, Temple had stressed that it was more important to copy the wisdom of the great men who provided such foundations rather than to mimic their acts.

The 300th Anniversary of 1904, which Francis presided over, was a great excuse for celebration. It was also the occasion for the noble institution of monitors to undergo reformation—and before some junior sprogg of today says "amen to that", we suggest he reads on carefully. There had been monitors at the School for generations, but they were by tradition the senior six boys of the classical sixth. The School Chaplain, a scholar from Shrewsbury, called Rev. C. G. Lowe, together with two monitors from the School House, worked out a new system where not only would the total number of monitors be increased, but the selection would be made from a wider field, based very much on leadership potential. Furthermore the monitorial powers, privileges and responsibilities were to be greatly increased. Monitors were to become far more responsible to the Headmaster for the discipline of the School. It must have sounded rather like a late twentieth century Chancellor's Budget to the junior boys, yet the system was a great success. The need to give the senior boys that level of responsibility has often been queried in more recent years amongst educationalists, yet are not girls of 18 for example, as trainee nurses, faced with heavier responsibility whilst they study? Lowe quoted Admiral Earl St. Vincent who was credited with having raised the discipline of the Navy to a high level prior to Nelson,

"The test of a man's courage is responsibility". Lowe keenly felt the need to prepare the senior boys for the exacting responsibilities and discipline that faced them in the administrative parts of the Empire, as well as for careers within the U.K. So much did he believe in the monitorial system, that when he died in 1929, there was in his Will a bequest that supplied money to furnish a room with "suitable dignity." for the monitors and also provide funds for a silver medal to be given to each School Monitor and a gold one for the Head of School. Lowe had maintained that the average schoolboy would respect and admire a strong monitor but would despise one who was weak.

Woodcut of School buildings

11
War

During the reign of Queen Victoria a military tradition was developing at Blundell's. By the late nineteenth century the School had its own Corps which was possibly linked to the local volunteers. There was inspiration for military careers as the Empire grew. The careers of Old Blundellians like General Sir George Tomykins Chesney, K.C.B. (OB 1835-1838) and General Sir George Malcome, G.C.B. (OB 1832-1833) read like adventure stories: served under Sir Charles Napier—to stop a charge of 1,500 Afghan horse—given command of a field force in the Indian Mutiny—served throughout the siege of Delhi—driving huge masses of their enemies in headlong riot—commander of a division in the Abyssinian expedition—foreign service. Yet there was another side to the coin, as shewn in the obituary notices in contemporary copies of *The Blundellain*.

"Nov. 1893—We much regret the death of Lieut. De Burgha Hodge of the Royal Welsh Fusiliers. He was in the School House from May '87 to Midsummer '91, and was gazetted to his regiment in Nov. 1893. He was taken ill at Oswestry with typhoid fever on May 11th. . . . The courage which made him a fearless rider in early boyhood, and a brilliant member of our eleven and fifteen, did not fail him in his last terrible illness. In mourning his loss we shall think of him with pride as one who could not have failed to win distinction had he been spared to see active service."

Nov. 1894—We record with great regret the death of Lieut. A. J. Holder OB, of the Durham Light Infantry, which took place very suddenly from heart disease on August 3rd, at Mhow, India. Lt. Holder was at Blundell's from 1883-1890. . . . He distinguished himself by

21.   P. K. PERKIN
Killed in Action, July 1st, 1916.

22.   A. L. SANDELL
(R.F.C.)
Killed in Action, April, 1917.

23. BLUNDELLIAN PRISIONERS
AT CREFIELD
Left to right as you look at them:

R. R. W. JACKSON, O.H.
A. S. HOOPER, WILTS., S.H.
D. H. GARDEN, BUFF., D.B.
H. W. C. LLOYD, WILTS., W.

24.   A. R. RENDELL, M.C.
(Capt. D.C.L.I.)
*Killed in Action, Macedonia,
Sept. 18th, 1918.*

". . . so gallant, so true hearted, so resolute but so terribly young. . ."

Blundell's School.

"*Pro patria populoque.*"

Situated at Tiverton, in Devon, the School was founded and endowed in 1604 by Master Peter Blundell, a clothier of that town. In 1882 new school premises were built a mile from the town, well in the country, and on high and open ground. The School figures in Robert Blackmore's famous novel, "Lorna Doone," John Ridd having been a boy at the School House. Blundell's numbers nearly 350. The illustration shows part of the front of the School, and the War Memorial, a carved Runic Cross which has been erected in front of the Chapel. In addition to the Cross, several Bursaries for the sons of Old Blundellians have been established. Rugby Football is the winter game, the School matches being with the R.N.C., Downside, Sherborne, Denstone, and Cranleigh.

25. & 25a. In 1927 Wills cigarettes published a series of 25 cigarette cards on public schools: Bedford, Blundell's, Bradfield, Bristol Grammar, Charterhouse, Cheltenham, City of London, Clifton, Eton, Haileybury, Harrow, Loretto, Malvern. Malborough, Merchant Taylor's (London), Mill Hill, Oundle, Repton, Royal Naval College, Dartmouth, Rugby, St. Paul's, Uppingham, Wellington, Westminster, Winchester.

26. J. W. E. Hall and F. R. Clayton at a School Fête in the 1950's.

winning the Russell three years in succession. . . . Of his career as an Officer, the regimental paper says: 'The service has lost a most promising officer, and the Regiment a valued comrade, whose presence will be daily missed at the mess table, on the cricket field, out shooting and at all manly sports and games.'

"Nov. 1897—With deep regret we have to announce the death of William Hubert Henry Smith, OB, (Westlake) Sept. 1885-1889. Modest and unassuming, he was beloved by boys and masters alike. He was a member of the famous "Invicti" XI, 1889, and was Captain of Football in his last season here. At RIE . . . he played regularly for the Rugby team . . . Capt. last season, . . . also played for Surrey County. Proceeding to India, his work lay on the Chenab Canal, Gujranwala, Punjab, where he died a few days ago."

"Dec. 1897—By the death of Lieut. Byron Henry Drury, 2nd West India Regiment, which occurred at Kingston, West Jamaica, on Nov. 11th, Blundell's has lost one of her most brilliant old boys and England a fine soldier. Nine years ago the name of "May" Drury was in every department of sport, one to conjure with. . . . He entered Blundell's S.H. 1883 and left in summer of 1889. . . . He entered the army in July 1891, was promoted to Lieutenant in May 1893, and was appointed garrison Adjutant at Sierra Leone in February 1895. He was invalided home, and while visiting his old School, playing for M.C.C. in 1896 (B. H. Drury, c. Spring b. H.G. Spring 86), he told the writer of this notice that the deadly climate of the West African coast had ruined his health. His untimely death, at the age of 27, reminds us of the loss of one who was his contemporary, though at another School. Newton College have by the death of Lieut. C. V. Windsor on the Indian frontier lost an old boy famous in all manly sport. We beg to offer Newton our sincere sympathy."

When the Boer War was over, more than 100 Old Blundellians had taken part in the hostilities—the memorial to those who fell is at the west end of the School Chapel. In the year of the tercentenary, 1904, the figures for entry into Sandhurst shewed Blundell's in third place behind Eton and Wellington College. A Special Army Class existed in the School to prepare candidates for entry into Woolwich and Sandhurst; others went direct to India. The Blundell's School Cadet Corps was formed as such in 1898 by Capt. E. F. C. Clarke and Capt. Peirce. The Corps was part of the Devon militia, equipped with the standard Lee-Enfield rifles and the inevitable bayonets. The School O.T.C. was formed in 1910. These were the days of putties and the Drill cup.

"I remember a certain Head of House who found himself faced with the training of a squad for the ever famous, but now forsaken, Drill cup. He hated O.T.C. and its drill most of all, and had not much brain power and no interest in strategy or tactics: indeed, on one of those glorious Field Days, for which the rest of the School got a half holiday, he was lining a hedge at the top of Newtes with his tired troops, and himself standing in a military attitude apparently working out the points of importance in the terrain from a map, when an Officer coming up and looking over his shoulder discovered that he was reading *Greenmantle*, then a popular novel. But to return to the training of his House squad. Each summer evening when the field rang with rattling bayonets and hoarse cries of command, he was noticed always to begin by sending his squad to march over the length of the field to the Old House; while they did this he studied the paragraphs of Infantry Training and so had the orders for the evenings manoeuvres soaked up as it were as a small sponge; he squeezed this out for the remaining time, and then returned to the House. Something attempted, something done. It all needed some nice calculation as to time, because I believe on one occasion the squad marched crossways from the gate and ended up in the Old House garden fence (not a secure structure) before the remaining paragraphs had been mastered, and the return orders remembered. His House eventually won the competition, owing perhaps a good deal to the shameless amount of 'Kiwi' allowed by the Housemaster on the bills to change the newly issued orange-leather equipment into a deep glossy brown, which it was said by the disappointed Houses, dazzled the eyes of the Judge so that he did not notice the mistakes in drill." (Granlund)

General Sir Douglas Gracey, K.C.B., K.C.I.E.,. C.B.E., M.C. Bar, I.C.S., M.A., Legion d'Honneur, Croix de Guerre et Plume, Commander in Chief Northern Command India and in 1948 Commander in Chief of the Pakistan Army. General Gracey went to School House and became Head of School just before the commencement of hostilities in the first Great War. He was born in 1894 and died in 1964. Another distinguished Old Blundellian soldier of that period was Major General James Elliott, C.I.E., (N.C. 1912. P. 1914-1915). General Elliott went direct to India from School and saw distinguished service on that sub-Continent, and became the author of several books on the history of the North-West frontier.

In 1914 before the commencement of hostilities there were nearly 240 Old Blundellians who were in the Colours and foreign parts, ninety eight of whom were in India and Ceylon. By November 1914, there were about 450 Old Blundellians already serving in the war. This figure grew to well over a thousand by 1918. First among those to fall were 2nd. Lieut. W. Bastard (NC 1905-10) aged 22, and 2nd. Lieut. Jasper Carew (SH 1908-12) aged 20.

> "But others were of high family, as any need in Devon, Carews, and Bouchiers, and Bastards. . . ." (from R. D. Blackmore's description of Blundell's School, in "Lorna Doone", chapter I).

They came from all over the world, from India, Canada, South Africa, New Zealand, Rhodesia, and not just from the Empire. There was for example, E. B. Hayden, an American (OH 1904-1908), who wrote to the Blundellian. (March 1917)

> "When war broke out, feeling the blood of my boyhood again course through my veins, I tried to enlist through the English Consul in Boston, but being a Yankee was not successful, so I did the next best thing; joined the American Ambulance, and came immediately to France. Have been in Belgium (1914-15) for ten months, went through the first and second battle of the Yser, the battle of Champagne and Verdun. At the latter place my nerves gave way, and I was in the hospital several weeks. Then I returned to America on a six weeks leave of absence, and collected $28,000 and sixty men for our corps.
>
> "Upon my return from the States I was decoratd with the Medal of Honour and War Cross so I feel I have in a small way upheld the honour of an OB, even though a Yankee."

In an earlier letter to a friend at Blundell's, Hayden wrote:

> "Should I come through all right, I intend to return to England and shall come down to mv old school, which is often in my thoughts."

Lieut. Edward Bartlett Hayden never was able to return to his old school, for he too was killed in battle.

The battlefields were often very different.
The Blundellian, 1916:

> "Second Lieut. P. K. Perkins whose loss was presumed in June last, is now known to have been killed on June 1st . . . he was in the second wave and was sent on to command the first. Twice wounded with bombs he continued to advance, and when unable to, he still cried "Come along lads." He was in his 23rd year."

The *Times:* Capt. D. Y. Garstin M.C., 4th Class Vladimir— (Postumous), (W. 1904-1909).

"In July of last year, on the 19th, the Bolshevists were in possession of Archangel. An expedition was on its way down the White Sea, with the intention of effecting a landing. Major-General Poole was in Murmansk, four or five hundred miles north, and with him was Colonel Thornhill. It was resolved to make an attempt to cut the railway at Oberserzki south west of Archangel, so as to hamper the retreat of the Bolshevists. . . . Just when the force was about to move away, Captain Denys N. Garstin, of the 10th Hussars, made his appearance. He came in rags and with health undermined, for he had made his escape from Moscow, hundreds of miles south, had walked most of the distance, and would have been sent home from Murmansk if he had reached the port. But he learned of the adventure towards Archangel, and begged Colonel Thornhill to include him in the party. At first the colonel refused, but Garstin insisted that with his knowledge of the country he might be of great assistance. He was taken. He proved his worth. Out here they speak of Garstin as a man worth while. He is asleep in the cemetery of Archangel, but he left behind a record of traditional valour."

Some were taken prisoner
From *The Times* Feb. 9th, 1917

Captain H. W. C. Lloyd, D.S.O., of the Wiltshire Regiment (W. 1907-10), who was taken prisoner in the autumn of 1914, has just returned to England after two years in the officers' prison camp at Crefeld, from which he escaped last month.

Last June Captain Lloyd, with a Russian officer, made an unsuccessful attempt to escape from Crefeld. They were court-martialled at Dusseldorf and sentenced to three months' imprisonment, not for attempting to escape, but for having cut their way through a cellar. The officers appealed against the sentence, and were ordered to go before a District Court-martial at Munster . . . .

. . . When the train halted at a junction Captain Lloyd escaped. He had worked out the details of the scheme previously, and they were based on experience gained on the occasion of his first visit to Munster. He proceeded to make his way across country in a north-westerly direction. He ran and walked all night (Captain Lloyd represented Cambridge in cross-country running in 1910-11-12), and at dawn reached a village which he recognised on the map. He hid all day in a big pine forest, and started again at night, travelling in a westerly direction.

Misled by a Band

At 1 o'clock the next morning he arrived at a village close to which was a fairly wide river, and as he passed through the streets he heard a band playing. This was the Kaiser's birthday, and he took it that the band was playing in honour of the event. Concluding that he was still in Germany, he retraced his steps, although the weather was bitterly cold, and on his way met two men who flashed torches in his face and asked him if he was a Russian soldier. He replied that he was not, and they then ordered him to go with them. They spoke in German, and he imagined that he was still in Germany until one of the men said, "You know you are in Holland, don't you?" . . . He spent that night in the guardroom, and on the next day went to hospital, as his feet were frost-bitten. To the bitterly cold weather which prevailed throughout his escape Captain Lloyd largely attributed his salvation. The frost was intense throughout, so much so that the trousers of his uniform froze stiff from the knee, and he had to cut them off with a knife.

Captain Lloyd states that while of late the food supplied at Crefeld has gradually gone from bad to worse, the treatment of the prisoners has improved to a corresponding degree. For the last year the prisoners, all officers, have had no butter or milk. There are just over 200 English officers in this camp, including two brigadier-generals; 400 French officers and 600 Russian officers. They have one good meal a day, which generally consists of soup and fish. On one day a week, however, they are given a small slice of meat and on Sundays they occasionally have pork. Captain Lloyd emphasises the fact that the British officers depend entirely on the parcels which come from England.

English people with friends at Crefeld will be relieved to know that the parcels arrive regularly. He believes that every parcel sent to him reached its destination. . . .

Some were in the Medical Corps

The Blundellian December, 1916: Capt. J. R. Merrick, M.C., R.A.M.C.

"I went up last Saturday (Nov. 12th) to a dug out, and spent nearly all day and night, until Friday, carrying in wounded. . . . The trenches were very wet and muddy, and even the bitter frost we had on Wednesday and Thursday night did not harden them.

During the later days, most of the nights were spent in taking up large bodies of men to carry wounded from German dug-outs. This was extremely hard work, as the ground was so cut up by the shells, but it improved later, when the ground got frozen . . .

. . . it had thawed during the day and rained heavily, so that it was very heavy going, and we several times had to pull men out of the mud. We only got near our place about 4-4.30 a.m. and then got very mixed up as to where we were. Just after we found someone to tell us where we were and where to go, one of our infantry officers and three of our men got wounded. Luckily they could walk, so we sent them home with the guides. Then as it was getting near daylight and the men were exhausted. . . ."

Others flew planes:

The Blundellian, November, 1917:

"Lieut. Roger Bolton Hay, M.C., West Yorkshire Regiment, attached R.F.C., was reported missing on July 17th, and subsequently news was received that he had died the same day that he had been taken prisoner by the Germans. He was at Blundell's (N.C.) from 1908-14, gaining football, cricket and gymnasium caps. He was proceeding to Oxford when the war broke out, and he joined the U.P.'s Brigade, afterwards obtaining a commission in the West Yorkshire Regiment. . . .

. . . In a letter his observer, Mr. G. O. Partington says, "Whilst flying near Ostend, my pilot and I somehow lost our formation and were attacked by six enemy scout aeroplanes. To start with, my gun jammed, and we were then pretty well helpless, and it was impossible to remedy it. We were a good many miles over the line, and my pilot made a really wonderful flight from 14,000 feet down to the ground. He looped, spun, and did everything he could to shake the enemy off; he was badly hit in the body towards the end, and had to land on the beach; we got out and I helped him along, when I was shot in the leg. It was awful luck, as we were only three or four hundred yards from our line."

Some were badly wounded, for example, 2nd Lieut. F. W. Hinings (N.C. 1900-06).

"His wounds are healing nicely, but he had an awful time of it. He was wounded (by shrapnel) in two places on his arm (in the upper arm the piece of shell went through into his side), right side of abdomen, and also right thigh. He also came in for some of the awful gas. Since he arrived at the hospital in London he has had pneumonia, pleurisy, and also a touch of malaria. At present his right arm is paralised. As soon as he is well enough they are going to operate and remove the piece of shrapnel which is still in his forearm. He is wonderfully cheery, and so amusing in spite of the pain and talks of 'when he goes back'."

He went back and was killed in action September 25th, 1916.

From *The Blundellian* March 1916:

Eric Ronald Wilson (D.B. 1904-08) of the Black Watch, has been mentioned in despatches and awarded the Military Cross "for gallant and distinguished service in the field" at Loos and Hill 70 on Sept. 25th. He was just 21 years old. He was badly wounded on Hill 70, but would not leave his men. He has since been gazetted Captain, as from Sept. 26th, 1915. He is now with his regiment doing duty in England, as he is not entirely recovered from his wounds . . . ."

Some died on the battle field in the closing stages of the war:
December 1918

"Captain Rendall's (M.C.) Company had to take a certain hill on the dawn of Sept. 18th. The hill was a small sugar loaf one, with practically no cover, and composed of rock which spintered easily—it was an excellent mark for the enemy. The hill was quite easily taken. . . . Unfortunately the men on the right failed to come up, and the Bulgars switched all their artillery on to this one hill, and for five hours the shell fire was awful. Captain Rendall was wounded almost at the beginning, but continued to organise the defence. He was wounded again, but still "carried on". the third wound was so severe that he died as he was being carried in."

Captain Rendall was tea-planting in Ceylon when he enlisted. He won the Russell Cup five years and the Mole Cup four years in succession when he was at school. He was also in the first XV and first XI. He was 26 when he was killed.

When O. F. Granlund wrote of his reminiscences of the first Great War, he possibly echoed the experiences of many such Masters in other Schools.

"At the end of the summer term of 1914, the three brothers Nind, (Willie, John and Ernest) who had been in Petergate under my predecessor G. H Norman, asked if they might come to stay in the House together. It was the first time since they had left the School that such a chance meeting all together in their old House had occurred. John, then a Captain in the Marines, seemed preoccupied, and he warned me that he might have to leave suddenly and without perhaps saying goodbye. He slipped away on the Sunday night, and we next heard of him in the North Sea. That must have been July 25th. During the same week-end Mons Letorey (French Master) disappeared from Tiverton. He was a staff interpreter in the French Army and we next heard of him riding as liaison-officer with the 9th Lancers in the brave but sickening disaster at Mons. I remember Letorey's graphic account of it which he gave me afterwards, and the horror of it. Then came the story of Birchall's escape from Berlin with his charming Polish wife and he went to the Army, and Hotblack and Rokeby and Batterbee".

". . . At Tiverton we were rather out of the war area, though of course we had food, cards and curtained windows in the Studies and Dormitories, and there was the Hospital at Knightshayes; we never saw an aeroplane until after the war was over. But term by term the stream of boys passed away, so gallant, so truehearted, so resolute, but so terribly young, and within a year so many we were never to see again. When Thornton died in 1916, and because Batterbee went to the Front, I became Army Class Master. I was also cricket Master, and these two tasks with the work as Assistant Chaplain gave me a strange mixed cup to drink, the keen companionship of jolly fun which absorbed us so fully because to be so short-lived, the wrestling with examination questions, and prayers, the clenching of the teeth as one read the daily lists, the poignancy, the pride, the drawn-out misery of it all. . . ."

. . . "Most of it comes back to me in small vivid pictures. I was travelling to London in December 1914, and read in "The Times" the death in action of Pryce-Jenkin (JH and OH 1907-1913). He and I had come to the School the same term, as boy and Master to the same form. Only two months before we had laughingly searched for a supposed burglar in the Petergate garden—funny that that incident should return—and now?! As I read his name I saw for the first time what a terrible cost of life the War was to mean."

"About two years later Harry Paddison (one of my four Blundellian brothers-in-law who went to the War) was killed. He had always been rather a special friend, and all the chivalry of War seemed to die with him—never again was it anything to me but something stark and grinding and loathsome. — stood with me under the trees in the garden in a thunderstorm, a very old friend, and once a colleague in the School. He hated war but had always prepared himself for it, and was a most efficient officer, and afterwards to be distinguished. He said to me, 'You know I hate war, but I can't help wanting to see how the machine I hace been training works in the field.' His words remain with me as a warning that groups of people cannot long collect the best and brightest of armaments always for use in dumb show, without some big rousing wish to let them off at one another's castles."

"After it was over I would never go to a War Film—is this cowardly? I hope not. But I have seen it, and felt it, all too vividly in imagination, with particular persons taking part, ever to want to see it in the Pictures."

The War Memorial outside the Chapel remembers the 200 Old Blundellians known to have been killed in that grim war, together with the 171 Old Blundellians known to have been killed in World War II. The total mortality from both wars was equivalent to the number of boys and Masters that were in the School during an average year of the first half of the twentieth century. Their names are on the School wall and the memorial cross is a reproduction of a Saxon cross in the Churchyard of Eyam, Derbyshire. Capt. E. C. Bellow (NC 1894-96), was the first Canadian to win a V.C. in the First World War.

Of the Masters, Mons Letorey returned with a bar to his Military Cross and was awarded the Croix de Guerre four times. Batterbee, Rokeby and Hotblack also returned, the last two with the Military Cross. A. L. Francis nearly lost a son when his ship went down, but Wynne lost his eldest son, killed in Mesopotamia two days before the Armistice. It was not a lovely war.

The cost to some individual families was dear:
The Blundellian February, 1917:

"Capt. Charles Robert Hay-Webb R.F.A. (N.C. 1908-1911) killed on December 22nd, aged 22 was the third and only surviving son of Mr. C. A. Hay-Webb of Mooktapore, Bihar, India . . . He went to the Front in January 1915, was severely wounded in the second battle of Ypres on April 30th, 1915 and was on medical leave for 11 months. He returned to the front in November. His elder brother, Captain Allan Benville Hay-Webb, died of wounds in Gallipoli in August 1915."

The Blundellian, November, 1917:

"Captain Henry Jepson Paddison M.C. (aged 21, D.B. 1910-15), Worcestershire Regiment, who was killed on August 16th, was the third son of Mr. Richard Paddison of Blundell's. Of the other brothers, the eldest has been seriously wounded twice, the second fell at Hooge on July 30th, 1915, while leading his company in a counter-attack, and the youngest is in a prisoner-of-war camp in Germany . . ."

We shan't see Willy any more, Mamie,
He won't be coming any more:
He came back once and again and again,
But he won't get leave any more....

And though you run expectant as you always do
To the uniforms we meet,
You'll never find Willy among all the soldiers
In even the longest street.

Nor in any crowd; yet, strange and bitter thought,
Even now were the old words said,
If I tried the old trick and said "Where's Willy?"
You would quiver and lift your head,

And your brown eyes would look to ask if I were serious,
And wait for the word to spring,
Sleep undisturbed: I shan't say *that* again,
You innocent old thing.

I must sit, not speaking, on the sofa;
While you lie asleep on the floor;
For he's suffered a thing that dogs couldn't dream of,
And he won't be coming here any more.

Excerpts from 'To a Bulldog' written by Sir John Squire, in memory of his brother Captain W. H. Squire (Acting Major), Royal Field Artillery, killed in 1917.

Four Epitaphs (from *The Times*)

From a general grave on Vimy Ridge.

> You come from England; is she England still?
> Yes, thanks to you that died upon this hill.
> ———
> 'Anglia vos misit; quid agit? Num vivit ut olim?'
> 'Hoc monte asperso sanguine vivit adhuc.'

On some who died early in the Day of Battle.

> Went the day well? We died and never knew;
> But well or ill, England we died for you.

Quis fuit eventus? Nescimus morte jacentes
Qualiscumque fuit, pro patria cadimus.

On those who died at the Battle of Jutland.
Proud we went down, and there content we lie,
'Neath English sea if not 'neath English sky.

―――

Nos mersit fluctus laetantes corda; Brittanni,
Si non terra tegit, nos tegit unda maris.

For a village War Memorial.
Ye that live on 'mid English pastures green,
Remember us, and think what might have been.

―――

Qui colitis terrae viridantia culta Britannae,
Tura date, hostili paene perusta manu.

A. L. Francis

From *The Blundellian* July 1920

Fit For Heroes.

"... A new world fit for heroes." The Prime Minister, 1918

Dawn is coming. We have preached it in the country of the Zulu,
    Guatemala, Honolulu,
    Beaconed from Trafalgar Square;
    I have seen our Erin burning
    With the Golden age returning,
And escaped from the Millenium they've started over there.

We have comrades in the Punjab, and must grin and bear them properly
    (Madras and Trichiopoly
    Have heard Trafalgar Square;)
    And they welcomed us as brothers
    (Vide Montagu and others).
They are seething with fraternity, say fugitives from there.

So if the claims of Liberty's high mission's unavailing,
    Then political blackmailing
    Must prove it from Above;
    For no matter where you scan it
    You'll find places on the planet,
Where weapons drip with brotherhood, and hands are red with love.

For we faced a mightly massacre to overthrow Autocracy,
    And save some other 'ocracy
    From gun, and sword and plot;
    If the world's not what we fought for,
    Nor as peaceful as we thought for,
Well, we've made it safe for something, though it isn't certain what.

                                                                                   Anon

12
'F'

A. L. FRANCIS retired in 1917 and died in 1925, the same year as the great Lord Curzon died and the centenary year of the birth of R. D. Blackmore. Affectionately known as 'F', he was greatly mourned. If Temple was the great Old Blundellian, surely Francis was a candidate for the title of the Great Headmaster. A man of many and varied talents, he could have even become an opera singer, the offer was made to him in his early days. The following is an extract from the sermon the School Chaplain Granlund preached at A. L. Francis' Memorial Service in 1926.

"What did he (Francis) really do? He built a new School for an old one, and he filled it with boys, and in doing this he 'asked counsel of both times', as Bacon says, 'of the ancient times what is best, and of the latter times what is fittest'.

"Would not all who worked under him say that Francis was always ready to sink his personal feelings, if he could by that means carry men united behind him, that he never intended for personal victory over the opinion of others, that he would always put the whole weight of his influence behind any convinced decisions of his friends; wasn't it just that set of qualities which led men to trust so much, and so rightly in the end, to the excellent spirit within the man, ay and this which shamed us younger men out of our own presumptions to follow more loyally when he had listened to our hesitations and interferences? And he was always ready to listen, especially when he saw a man ruffled and upset, and then would presently come the slowly stirring smile which drew the gritty growth out of our own eyes with the power of a magnet. Trifles sometimes strangely annoyed him, but it was generally because he felt they were symptoms of something bad beneath."

Francis had been Headmaster of Blundell's for 43 years. He had not used the School as a spring board for higher preferment, as he could most easily have done, but having a vision for the place, devoted his life to seeing it through.

Granlund observed that there was an "unselfconscious naturalness of his Christian faith." Although the first Headmaster of the School not to be in holy orders, he wrote two hymns. The first he composed for the tercentenary of the School, this hymn being sung also at the Pan-Anglican Festival at St. Paul's Cathedral, being selected out of an entry of 5,000. This is a wonderful hymn of praise, which recognises man to be God's crowning work (rather than just a 'naked ape'.) This commemoration hymn is sung each year at the Old Boys' service. The second hymn Francis wrote was by request for the tercentenary of the Borough of Tiverton in 1915.

COMMEMORATION HYMN

(as adapted for the Thanksgiving Service at St. Paul's, June 24th 1908—from *The Blundellian,* June 1908)

Great Lord of wisdom, life and light,
Before the hills were founded,
Thy quickening breath dissolved the night
And stirred through deeps unsounded.
Beneath Thy hand the formless earth
And ocean rolled asunder,
And in Thy likeness man had birth,
Thy crowning work and wonder.

Through that grey dawn Thou calledst him,
Untaught but not unheeding;
His feet were faint, his lamp was dim,
Yet Faith discerned Thy leading.
Age after age and line on line
Thy Book unfolded clearer,
Till, like a flush of morn divine,
Thy Son proclaimed Thee nearer.

His Word from East to slumbering West
Went out for all creation;
Our far-off islands woke and blessed
Thy name with adoration.
We kneel where our forefathers knelt,
They trod these courts before us;
Unseen, though near, our hearts have felt
Their blessings wafted o'er us.

We thank Thee, Lord, for these our sires,
Whose faith, in power out-welling,
Through flood, through field, through martyr fires,
Hath wrought by love compelling.
Still breathe on us, great Lord of morn,
That zeal of Saints and Sages;
So tongues unheard and isles unborn
Shall hymn Thy praise through ages.

We bless Thy Name for one and all,
Who founded for Thy glory
Each low-built shrine, each minster tall,
To teach mankind Thy story.
May we, their sons, our lamp display
Of love and wisdom burning,
Till twilight melt in golden day
At our dear Lord's returning.

        A. L. Francis, M.A., Headmaster of Blundell's School

    Francis House was named after A. L. Francis, and was opened in great style in 1926 by both Lords Temporal and Spiritual, though the firm that built it unfortunately went bankrupt in the process. Officially Lord Fortescue the then Lord Lieutenant of Devon, had been asked to do the actual honours, *i.e.,* open the boys' door with a silver key, make an impromptu speech, and ask on the spur of the moment for an extra half holiday for the boys; but Bishop Lord Cecil of Exeter, who was invited to give just a blessing, was not it appears in the habit of playing second fiddle to a mere Peer of the Realm, and to the astonishment of the organisers, seemed to take over the whole ceremony. Splendidly robed, he anticipated Lord Fortescue by giving a magnificent speech, then smiting the doors with his staff declared the house verily open in the name of the Holy Trinity, leaving the bewildered Peer to wonder if there were any lines left for him—save the asking for the extra half holiday, which the Bishop had generously omitted to include in his own performance.

    Before the lovely garden and trees were planted, by its first Housemaster Vernon Clough, Francis House looked indeed stark and modern among the mellow setting of the rest of the School, and soon received the nickname of the 'Jam Factory' from its rival Houses. The story goes that a local 'bus conductor with a distorted sense of humour once directed a tramp to Francis House having convinced him that it was the local workhouse.

Perhaps one of the most distinguished Old Blundellians who was at Blundell's during the time of Francis was Prof. A. V. Hill, C.H., O.B.E., F.R.S., D.Sc., L.L.D., M.D., Associate Member of the Académie Royale de Belgique, etc., (D.B. 1900-1905). On leaving Blundell's he went to Trinity College, Cambridge where he was third wrangler in 1907 and fellow from 1910-1916. In 1927 he was awarded the Nobel Prize for Medicine and Physiology jointly with Otto Meyerhoff for his discovery relating to the production of heat in muscles. He was M.P. for Cambridge from 1940-1945, a Governor of Blundell's from 1919-1944 and President of the O.B. Club from 1964-1977. He died on 3rd June, 1977, aged 90.

From *The Blundellian* February 1917.

Impressions of English Weather, by a wounded ANZAC

It rained, and rained, and rained, and rained,
The average was *well* maintained,
And when our lawns were simply bogs,
It started raining cats and dogs.
After a drought of half-an-hour,
There came a most refreshing shower—
And then, the strangest thing of all,
A gentle shower began to fall.
Next day we had it *fairly* dry,
Save for a deluge from the sky,
That wetted people to the skin,
And *after* that the rain held in.
Folks wondered about what *next* they'd get,
They got, in fact, a lot of wet;
But soon we'll have the change again,
And perhaps we'll get a drop of rain.
                    (From the Chronicles of the N.Z.E.F.)

13

Rev. Arthur Edward Wynne (Headmaster 1917-1930)

WYNNE was the last Headmaster to date to have been promoted from within the School. It was probably during his time that Blundell's gained the reputation of being an extremely tough and highly disciplined School, more so than in the days of Hughes and Francis. These were the days when the Viginti Club was formed.

From *The Blundellian* June 1926

Viginti Club

The above named club was formed last term. Membership, limited to twenty, is restricted to:

    a) School Monitors, *ex-officio*.
    b) Members of the School teams and Upper Sixth standing, who have distinguished themselves in the service of the School.

E. T. Benson	C. G. Stowell
L. G. Newton	A. S. Crawley
J. W. Stephens	A. J. C. Block
H. S. Robinson	D. A. K. W. Block
N. C. Phillips	C. L. Ashford
A. Biss	F. Lord
D. J. Fountaine	J. W. S. Blake
J. K. McIntyre	R. H. V. Reed
E. H. Densham	D. W. Price
J. R. Croggan	R. J. Eustace

In *Bluff Your Way in Social Climbing,* John Walker describes a Public School in the following manner.

"Public School binds Society together. An exclusive boarding school forms such a perfect closed environment for keeping the rest of the world at a decent distance that many men devote their lives to recreating the atmosphere of their youth in such places as London clubs. Certainly, they never recover from the triumphs and horrors of their five years at boarding school. They spend the twilight of sixty years reminiscing over their brief moment of glory as a prefect."

The subsequent life and careers of the original members of the Viginti Club make nonsense of that statement, as a quick glance through the OB records would indicate. E. T. Benson went on to Oxford getting a Blue at Cricket (wicket-keeper), and Rugby (scrum half) and played in the MCC tour of New Zealand 1929-30. C. L. Ashford, after obtaining his rugger blue in 1929, followed a distinguished legal career. L. G. Newton, a former running blue, is now Sir George Newton. J. W. Stephens is now Brigadier J. W. Stephens, D.S.O. Lieut. Col. Neville Cantley Phillips died in 1976 at Sandhurst, and Lieut. Col. Amyss Biss died in 1975. J. K. McIntyre, who played Rugby for Blackheath and the Army before changing over to the R.A.F., is now Air Commodore Kenneth John McIntyre, C.B., C.B.E., J.P. Air Vice Marshall Cuthbert Gordon Stowell died in 1975. The Block twins (who incidentally played Rugby for Sandhurst), are now Major General A. D. C. Block, C.B., C.B.E., D.S.O., and Brigadier D. A. K. W. Block C.B.E., D.S.O., M.C. J. R. Croggan won a Cross country Blue at Cambridge and D. W. Price ran for the Army, and broke a record at Fenners, and so on.

During this time three young Masters joined Blundell's, who were to give the School so much during their times there. T. R. K. Jones ('Jonah') came in 1922 and taught for 37 years, R. G. Seldon ('Ronnie') came in 1924 and taught for 40 years, and A. R. B. Thomas ('Bundy') in 1926, taught for 43 years. Colin Beale (S.H. 1925-1930 and School Bursar 1953-1973) clearly remembers A. R. B. Thomas coming to the School and opening up the world of trigonometry in a vivid new way for some of the more reluctant scholars. By taking them all out of the classroom and by pointing a theodolite at Old House he shewed some very practical aspects of what they were trying to learn, This was a new concept for the boys, for up to then the instruments they had thought of pointing at Old House were probably only obtainable from the School armoury. Not many years after this incident, Colin Beale, as a Naval Officer during World War II, recalled with thanks that clear teaching by 'Bundy' at Blundell's that had thoroughly grounded him for the exacting calculations he was having to do at sea. 'Bundy' himself, who taught during the reign of six Headmasters, gave Old Blundellians during the 1975 O.B. Dinner held in his honour in London, a delightful account of some of the earlier years.

". . . "Fusty" Wynne was my first (Headmaster), and in his thirteen years (1917-1930), much building went on: Francis House, the Hospital, the Pavillion, workshops, fives courts, houses in Tidcombe Lane for the staff. His other contribution was to the discipline of the place. I was interested to read in the current number of *The Blundellian* that "talking during lessons is permitted, within reason of course, and also the speaking of one's mind." I thought of my first term at Blundell's in 1926; I had been teaching in what was, I think, room 27 (for many years subsequently a Dayroom for Milestones), and 'Fusty' was teaching in the small classroom beneath (until recently the Bursar's Office). He sent for me later on and told me that, while he had been teaching, he had distinctly heard a boy in my class shuffle his foot on the floor. He told me that if such conduct continued I should have to leave Blundell's, so nobody moved his feet in future in my classes. 'Fusty' also visited the classrooms on the most absurd pretexts, but once he had decided that the master was O.K. he left him alone. Under his Headship Blundell's was a heavily disciplined School, a state of affairs that did not alter much until Gorton's Headship (1934-43).

"Ross Wallace was Headmaster for a mere four years, that included the Great Depression. Blundell's was feeling the effects of this, and I remember Wallace startling the Common Room by saying suddenly 'Gentlemen, this isn't business.' Until his remark nobody had thought it was. R. L. Roberts (1943-1948) told the School at the very first Big School that he had come to make them 'braced and compact'. He also halted the dismissal of the School to ensure that there was no talking while he gave his Dismissal Orders. The Orders in question were 'Sixth Form' and 'Lower School'. Between the two there was usually a buzz of conversation which he abolished.

"Jack Carter and John Stanton ushered in an era of progress with tranquility, with occasional ripples of discontent from the 'progressives' during John's Headship. I remember the latter very kindly. He was away on holiday in August, 1967, when news of my forthcoming marriage in the School Chapel came to a startled Blundell's. John immediately got in touch and offered Blundell House for our guests. It was a most kind offer; we accepted it, and put up 11 guests there, in addition to the bridegroom. John cared very much for flowers, and the rose beds and flowering shrubs around the Chapel and School Buildings came from his caring."

A. R. B. Thomas also recalled the Housemasters of the 1920's during his speech.

..."To begin with, the Housemasters owned their Houses, and were thus a mighty power in the School and couldn't be thrown out. This lasted until just before the 1939-1945 War, when the Housemasters were quite glad to sell out to the School as they were no longer making the large profits to which they had grown accustomed. It was said (with what truth I know not) that the breakeven point for a Housemaster was 42 boys in the House, below this he lost money.

". . . Some Housemasters kept pigs, which fed on boys' leavings. 'Cabby' Fisher varied this in School House by keeping bees that regularly swarmed on the School lime trees. Fifty years ago it was known to be hopeless to try ringing up a Housemaster at 7.30 in the evening; at that hour he was in his bath prior to dressing for dinner. In the summer term Quiet Hour (as it was not then called) was from 8 to 9 at night, and the boys mainly played with balls on Big Field, Cornwall's (later Gornhay) or Mayfield. Rounders was the favourite game and, soon after 8.30, Housemasters, resplendent in evening dress, would take the air together on Big Field. It was a noble sight.

"Each House had its tradition. School House, as Colin (Beale) well knows, had the best food. Each day at lunch the House was offered a choice of three main dishes, today's roast, yesterday's cold, or the day before's stew, mince or curry. Petergate was not so fortunate, and the queue that waited for the tuckshop to open usually contained several from Petergate, a House that was divided into three parts, neither part being allowed to speak to the other without special permission. This was also the case in North Close until after the War. One other School House tradition was the speed at which fags answered fag-whistles around the rectangled bends of the House corridors. This was said to maintain the House tradition of jinking three-quarters and fly-halves.

"Another relic of those far-off days was the custom of Housemasters sharing out among themselves the home cricket matches, each House giving a Garden Party. As soon as the tea interval arrived, a procession slowly wended its way from the Pavilion to the particular House.

"Other changes in the last 50 years are Chapel services and Roll-call. In those days there were three services every Sunday, Matins and Evensong being complusory for staff as well as boys. The School had three chaplains, Oscar Granlund, Vernon Clough and Robert Abigail with a fourth one John Andrews, on the way. Roll call was taken at 4 o'clock on every half-holiday beneath the Tower, until abolished by Gorton.

"Porterage was a charge made on each House account for the services of the House man, who met parents at the beginning and end of term and helped with the luggage. All boys had wooden geometry boxes which were used to record the number of beatings—a kind of status symbol. Other, and better, status symbols, were the Fire Brigade and the Viginti Club; if you belonged to either you had definitely made the grade. The Fire Brigade practised with a length of hosepipe and a crude pumping arrangement. It was actually called out many years ago to fight a fire in the Town, without much success, but with grateful thanks. It was killed off by the War and by the stirrup pump. Only real bloods belonged to the Viginti Club, which performed sketches and very bad pop music; it was killed off by Gorton.

"How many of you remember the Black Maria, that peculiar enclosed vehicle in which a boy with a temperature was wheeled to the School Hospital? It was superseded by the Housemaster's car, but was again used in the War when there was no petrol.

"Fifty years ago the Town was different, too. The streets were not tarmacadamed, and got very slushy in winter. A cab driven by Mortimer went from the Palmerston to meet every train. There were more pubs than now, although there are still a lot, and they were taboo to Masters, although the younger ones went to the Palmerston for a drink. Picture their surprise, when Mr. Peirce, speaking on behalf of the Housemasters, said it was not seemly for a Blundell's Master to be in the bar of the Hotel.

"Fifty years ago there was a rivilry between the breweries of Tiverton and Wiveliscombe, owned respectively by Starkey, Knight and Ford, and Arnold and Hancock. Most of the Tiverton pubs (some 20 of them) belonged to one brewery or the other, and I remember distinctly that Jonah had a preference for Arnold and Hancock. Controversy about the quality of the beers in Tiverton became so fierce that, at length, it was ended when a bottle of each beer was sent (with labels removed, simply marked 'A' and 'B') to the Public Analyst for his verdict. It soon came, and was totally unexpected. 'Neither horse should be worked for a month'."

It would seem that Arthur Wynne believed in the tradition of Headmasters of Blundell's living to grand old ages. He holds the School record, which we trust will yet be broken, dying in 1966 in his 101st year, surviving the champagne party given in his honour by former staff and pupils. Major General J. G. Elliott recalls the occasion of the London O.B. Dinner in 1929 when the poet, Sir John Squire (S.H. 1901-1903) was in the chair. In his speech, Sir John accidentally kept referring to Mr. Wynne as "Mr. Gwynne". Wynne, in his reply, politely thanked "Mr. Choirs" for his kind comments . . . During his time at Blundell's, Wynne was ordained.

Service in the Empire by Old Blundellians was often reflected in the King's Birthday Honours of that period.

1926

C.I.E. Miles Irving, O.B.E., I.C.S. (DB 1885-1894) Financial Secretary to the Government of Punjab.

C.I.E. John Bernard Collard Drake, O.B.E., I.C.S. (W. 1898-1902). Secretary to the High Commissioner of India.

C.B.E. (Military) Lieut. Col. Charles Richard Palmer Landon D.S.O. (NC. 1891-1897). Commanding 10th/20th Burma Rifles.

In 1926, out of the 600 members of the O.B. Club, 250 were filling or had filled positions of responsibility in the overseas Dominions and Colonies.

In 1929 there were 33 Old Blundellians working in Ceylon alone, and in *The Blundellian* of June 1930 the following were mentioned in *Old Blundellian News*.

"Sir Denys de Saumarez Bray, K.C.I.E., C.S.I., C.B.E., lately Foreign Secretary of the Government of India, has been awarded the K.C.S.I.

C. H. Harper, C.M.G., O.B.E., Governor and Commander-in-Chief of St. Helena, has been awarded the further Honour of K.B.E.

G. A. S. Northcote, Chief Secretary of Northern Rhodesia, has been appointed Colonial Secretary of the Gold Coast.

We are glad to record that Major E. L. Farley, M.C., R.E., who with another British Officer and his wife, was kidnapped on the road near Quetta on June 4th and carried over the frontier, was released unharmed on June 7th.

Blundellians will follow with interest the future career of G. F. P. Benson who has already made his mark at the Royal Academy of Dramatic Art having taken his Diploma and won the Silver Medal. Among other prizes he had been awarded Lady Tree's Prize for Elocution."

During Mr. Wynne's time the School was arranged into three parallel streams, Classical, Mathematical, and Modern. The Junior House was abolished in 1925. In January 1918 the School reached the 300 level for the first time and by the time Mr. Wynne retired, there were about 350 boys on the register.

Among those educated at Blundell's under Wynne were General Sir Walter Walker, K.C.B., C.B.E., D.S.O. (D.B. 1926-31), Brig. Sir Robert Arundell, C.M.G., O.B.E. Former Governor of the Windward Islands (N.C. 1918-23) The Revd. Professor Geoffrey Lampe, M.C., D.D., F.B.A. (D.B. 1926-31), former Regius Professor of Divinity at Cambridge, the Lord Stokes of Leyland (F.H. 1927-31) and the current president of the Old Blundellian Club, His Grace the Duke of Somerset (S.H. 1924-30). Also Air Vice Marshall Howard Ford, C.B., C.B.E., A.F.C. (W. 1920-25) and Rear-Admiral Richard Paige, C.B. (S.H. 1925-29).

The Tivvy Bumper

A book on Blundell's would not be complete without some mention of that cheerful little engine that used to regularly clank its way past the School parade ground. This account was written during Wynne's time.

The Blundellian, July 1929:

As we take our last look round the School and its environs we say to ourselves. "What is there above all else connected with Blundell's that is permanent, that will never change, as the old order is apt to do?" And the answer comes at once: "Why, of course, that age old institution, whose characteristics and eccentricity are so briefly epitomized by the words 'The Tivvy Bumper.' " This vehicle, conveyance or whatnot has provided many a budding poet with a theme and now it serves us for inspiration. What one notices primarily is its friendly habit of waiting for all and sundry, no matter how long overdue. For instance, we were the other day peacefully sleeping in an uncomfortable corner of it, while it waited for the word of command to proceed, in the fond hope that we should be only a quarter of an hour, or, at the most, twenty minutes late at the other end. Suddenly a voice was heard saying that her friends would only be a minute or two now. Did the guard blow the whistle and start? No not he: courteously he stood by her for the next five minutes while she waited, telling her that he positively could not wait a second longer. The first half of the journey was spent in the dear old lady telling everyone in the carriage twice, and privileged friends four times, what actually happened. Perhaps the most exciting moment is caused when a passenger forgets to alight at a station. When the train is eventually stopped and the unfortunate extracted, it exhibits one of its other powers, namely, in times of stress, of having to go backwards before going forwards: this we believe has something to do with perpetual motion or the absence of it. Thus it goes on with steady determination, stopping only between stations when it feels inclined: its driver, stoker and guard are cool and collected men; they have had experience on wilder and more abandoned lines such as the Tiverton Junction to Hemyock branch. It is the one permanent feature of the landscape, thanks to the burghers of Tiverton, who refused to have the main line through the town. It has plied to and fro for many generations, bringing new boys and taking away old boys and we suppose and hope that it will go on doing so for years to come. We shall be leaving by it within the next few days; let us hope that it will not be more than a quarter of an hour late, or, at the most, twenty minutes.

And poetry of the period:

From *The Blundellian* December 1929

The New Boy

I saw him as he lingered there,
A little boy with tumbled hair
Regarding with defiant air
The world around.

I watched him as he scratched his cheek
And blew his nose, as though to seek
Diversion in a world so bleak
As he had found.

I followed as, with careless gait,
He sauntered. Now appeared to wait
A friend who seemingly was late,
Poor friendless child!

He smiled as though he didn't mind
The strangeness and the words unkind,
He blinked to hide the tears behind,
E'en while he smiled.

I didn't think the worse of you,
You little boy, who seemed so new,
Because you wist not what to do,
And looked so naive.

But thought that you, who lingered there
With freckled face and troubled hair,
Pretending that you didn't care,
Were rather brave.

J. L. Taylor (N.C. 1926-30)
(also Captain of Cricket)

The boy who walked into the Common Room in break.

14

Rev. Alexander Ross Wallace (Headmaster 1930-34)

A R. WALLACE was the son of Major General Sir Alexander Wallace, K.C.B. Born in India in 1891, educated at Clifton and Corpus Christi, Cambridge (he was president of his college boat club), Wallace came to Blundell's having already done distinguished service in India as a Magistrate, and then Deputy Commissioner of Lucknow. Before his Blundell's appointment he was assistant master at Wellington College, and then headmaster of Carglefield School, near Edinburgh.

Before Mr. Wallace had been long at the School, new School Clubs were being formed, the Geographical Society (started by Mr. W. French), the Black and White Club (to foster the Arts), and the Apollo Club (artistic appreciation), and in 1932 the Cavendish Club (social concern) was resurrected. The Literary Club and the Viginti Club continued to flourish as did a very strong Music Club, which by 1930 had already given 22 concerts, for example:

Programme for 21st Concert. 1930

1. "This is the Record of John" Orlando Gibbons (1583-1625) R. H. P. Seymour, J. M. Draper, W. F. P. Greenslade, U. V. Smith, O. S. Fisher.
2. Verse anthem "The Peaceful West Wind" Campion.
    Song "Flow not so fast, ye fountains" (Downland 1563-1626) Mrs. J. W. E. Hall.
3. Harmonised Ayre for five voices "Awake, Sweet Love" Dowland.
    R. H. P. Seymour, J. M. Draper, W. F. P. Greenslade, U. V. Smith, O. S. Fisher.
4. Harmonised Anthem for five voices
    "Ave Verum Corpus" from five-part Mass Wm. Byrd (1542-1637) Mrs. J. W. E. Hall, J. M. Draper, B. R. Feaver, J. W. E. Hall, Esq., A. R. B. Thomas, Esq.
5. Ballad for five voices "Now is the Month of Maying" Morley (1567-1603)
    R. H. P. Seymour, J. M. Draper, W. F. P. Greenslade, U. V. Smith, O. S. Fisher.

6. Harmonised Polyphonic Anthem for four voices
   "Let Thy Merciful Ears, O Lord" Weelkes (1576-1603)
   R. H. P. Seymour, J. M. Draper, W. F. P. Greenslade, U. V. Smith, O. S. Fisher.

7. Polyphonic Madrigal for four voices
   "Adieu, Sweet Amarylis" Wilbye
   Mrs. J. W. E. Hall, J. M. Draper, B. R. Feaver, J. W. E. Hall, Esq. A. R. B. Thomas, Esq.

The Blundellian, December 1930 comments:

"Early English Music, with special reference to the Tudor School. Concert given by W. E. R. Townsend and J. C. Goodman.

"After Handel, except for a few isolated stars, England ceased to be a land of composers. With the possible exception of Purcell, however, Byrd was the greatest composer England ever knew. It is surprising how little of his music and that of other Tudor composers is now published. This concert was much appreciated by the Club, being upon a subject somewhat new to them."

There was also a Bach Choir which was trained by Mr. J. W. E. Hall. They performed the B Minor Mass in 1931. The Debating Society also continued to stimulate healthy and lively argument as it had done in previous years:

1914 That this House disapproves of the modern form of dress.

1914 That in the opinion of this House, the Abolition of War would be disastrous to civilisation.

1914 That the growing popularity of illustrated papers and magazines in a sign of the degeneracy of the present age.

1915 That this House considers the present censorship of war news too severe.

1918 That in the opinion of the House, Germany has had, and still has, more resources of brain power than any other nation.

1919 That Polar Expeditions benefit the community.

1920 That this House would welcome the abolition of Capital Punishment.

1920 That this House considers the League of Nations is detrimental to the British Empire.

1921 That in the opinion of this House, Britannia should rule the clouds rather than the waves.

1921 That this House would welcome communication with Mars.
1922 That this House would welcome Prohibition.
1922 That this House considers the cinema to have an evil influence.
1922 That this House would welcome the abolition of titles.
1925 That in the eyes of the schoolboy, bachelor Uncles are preferable to maiden Aunts.
1927 This House views with alarm the prospect of the flappers' vote.
1929 In the opinion of the House, Polar Exploration is useless and foolish.
1929 That this House opposes a scheme for the United States of Europe.
1930 That this House views with alarm the rapidly increasing power of women in public affairs.
1931 That this House hates Highbrows.
1931 In the opinion of this House, England is going to the dogs.
1931 This House deplores the modern phase of record breaking.
1932 In the opinion of this House, newspapers are debasing public tastes.

What was Blundell's like in the Thirties? There is a brief description given by Sir John Squire in *The Honeysuckle and the Bee.* Chapter One sets the scene.

" 'Well, why don't you?' said she.

I had just remarked that the way I should really like to take a holiday would be by going through the South and West of England on a horse. I had, I said, when young, done a very great deal of walking in those parts. I had regualarly walked home from Cambridge to Devonshire, and, later on, I had done several long walks with nothing in my pocket except what I had picked up by cutting people's grass or holding horses' heads. Then, after the war, for years after the war, I had escaped the urban pressure in a car and investigated inns and churches and just rung up anybody I knew within driving distance for a bed for one night. But cars, I said, go too fast, and have to be driven, and tempt one to go too far. And, on foot, I said, one sometimes gets impatient with dull country, and annoyed because one cannot see over the hedges. 'A horse,' I said, 'would be the ideal thing; a horse at a walking pace with just an occasional trot.'

'Well, why don't you?' said she.

'All sorts of reasons,' I replied. 'For one thing I don't suppose that nowadays you could get a horse put up in this country. When I was young every country pub had 'Good Accommodation for Man and Beast' written up on it. The sign might well still stand as half the motorists are beasts, but they don't expect horses now and they'd be staggered if one presented them with one. The modern innkeeper probably doesn't even know what horses eat.'

'Nonsense,' said she, 'they'd always be able to give your horse a shake-down somewhere and you could always get provender from a neighbouring farmer.'

'Perhaps you're right,' said I, 'but the drawback is that I haven't got a horse.'

'Can't you buy one?' she exclaimed impatiently.

'That's precisely what I can't do,' I said, 'because I can't afford it,'

'Then,' she rejoined with the logic of her sex, 'why don't you take a holiday on foot, writer a book about it, and buy a horse with the proceeds?'

'And then,' I continued, 'take a holiday on the horse, write a book about it and buy a Rolls-Royce with the proceeds. And then take a holiday in the Rolls, write a book and buy a steam-yacht (which I've always wanted) with the proceeds and then. . .'

I was interrupted.

'Don't dodge,' said she. 'It would do you all the good in the world to go off on foot again. As a matter of fact, I don't believe you could.'

That is the way one is made to do things. 'Can't I?' thought I. But what I said was: 'I daresay a little solitude would do me good, and I shall start off on Monday.' That is precisely what I did.

But first I had to decide where to go. And then I thought: 'Why not walk home to Devon as you used to do?' And then, my mind wavering over that varied country, which seemed in youth so illimitable, thinking of Dartmoor, Exmoor, the Tavy Valley, Bideford Bridge, the grey moorland churches, the rich fabrics of Ottery and Cullompton, I thought suddenly of my old school, Blundell's, within four miles of that last. It would be empty and I would go there for an hour or two, wander about, and recover the past.''

...Page 265

"I walked past the playing-fields and the houses. I passed the Chapel and Big School. I wanted to go in by the main gates.

I went in. There was nobody about. The square tower still stood there, its red sandstone as calm and kind as ever; and the great high trees on their lawns on the hither side of it, and the long line of mullioned windows, sunlit or blue-bough-shadowed, stretching away to the right, and the Chapel far back on the left, with a new memorial cross in front of it that had no need to be there in my time.

There was no sound from beyond the roofs of a ball being kicked or bumping, no echoes of the old cries of "Take it with you forwards," no distant shrillness of whistle.

The stones and leaves were the same. Other boys would be there in a month. The man who used to blow the whistle would be there no more.

A mist came in front of me and I saw forms long dead or strayed. Boys swarmed up the drive in strange bowler hats. Boys ran out at the news of motor-cars. Boys sat late in their studies making coffee. Boys told stories to each other in dark dormitories, creepy stories which made them spring up with stopped hearts when strange wailings came from gas-meter or radiator. Fags came back from farms loaded with eggs, cream and flowers. People over beyond the Tower played fives. Others were in the tuck-shop. And Willy was there.

* * *

I pulled myself up. It was I that had changed. The old things would endure. Even now there were boys who would return thirty years hence and not a stick or stone would have altered. Only themselves. Less merry, less confident, with older hearts and knowing too late the meaning of words that sounded empty to boyish ears: "if youth but knew." And sad will be the song within them if they come as I, when the place is empty. It is better to come when there is distraction.

I found someone who let me into School House. I went down the zigzagging corridor past studies with strange names on the doors, and at last, feeling like a burglar, opened the door of the one at the end, which was ours.

Some of the chairs seemed to be familiar. Football and cricket groups did not seem to be so much in favour as of old. There was little difference in the books on the shelves; the fevers of London seemed to have left this study at least unscathed. Whatever photographs of handsome mothers, plump sisters, and fathers in uniform there may have been had been stored away in cupboards.

There wasn't much to see. And then I suddenly remembered. With a pocket-knife (for the yellow dressing stone was almost as soft as the red sandstone) I had carved my name on the window-sill. Could it still be there?

It was, I could read "J.C.SQ"; and a few strokes were still visible after it."

Wallace's brief stay at Blundell's included the days of the Great Depression. He moved across to Dorset to become Headmaster of Sherborne.

TAKING AN EXAMINATION IN "BIG SCHOOL": CERTIFICATE CANDIDATES AT WORK. THE MAIN BLOCK OF SCHOOL BUILDINGS COMPRISES CLASS-ROOMS, THE LIBRARY AND "BIG SCHOOL." WEST OF THIS ARE THE SCIENCE BUILDINGS, LECTURE ROOMS, AND A BIOLOGICAL LABORATORY.

The Illustrated London News Picture Library

15

The Rt. Rev. Neville Vincent Gorton (Headmaster 1934-1942)

WHEN the Rev. Gorton came to Blundell's from Sedbergh, he brought with him two Masters who were closely connected with Sedbergh and were to greatly influence Blundell's. D. A. Rickards, a former pupil at Sedbergh, came to Blundell's with a fine athletic record. He had won the ten-mile cross country race for three successive years at Sedbergh and was a Cambridge three miler and first home for Cambridge in the 1934 University Cross Country race. Rickards' time at Blundell's was interrupted by a distinguished War record, and he finally left the School in 1953 to be the first Headmaster of Welbeck, the new army sixth-form College. The other Master that Gorton brought with him from Sedbergh was William Lyons Wilson. Gorton had some very advanced educational ideas for his time, and the world of Art and Music had been rather 'non-U', especially amongst some of the Viginti set, and Gorton had set himself the task to redress this deficiency. Lyons Wilson's brief included not only the practical instruction of Art but to introduce a new compulsory subject into the Lower School called Art Appreciation. Here Lyons Wilson manfully strove, aided by his famous epidiascope, to lift the rather sports-orientated minds of his class on to the level of higher and more beautiful things. A lesser man would have easily given up, but although some of the pupils may have appreciated certain of Titian's works for the wrong reasons, to others a new world of colour, shadow and design was opend up. The possession of a Lyons Wilson water colour is considered a great privilege and joy by people who may know little about the School where the artist taught. Some time ago, Lyons Wilson was greatly delighted to read his own obituary in a book on Yorkshire artists kindly lent to him by A. R. B. Thomas, and like Mark Twain of old he could claim that this account of his death was an exaggeration. Apparently the author had despatched him some time in the 1950's. Sadly W. E. Lyons Wilson died in the Summer of 1981.

Arthur Mee described the alterations to the School Chapel that Gorton instituted in the Devon Volume of his work on the 'King's England';

"It would have pleased old Peter Blundell to see the boys of his School at work in their new buildings. It happened that extensions to the Chapel of the School had the effect of removing the altar too far from the congregation, and certain alterations were necessary, architectural and structural, to overcome this. The Chapel, by a special arrangement, belongs to the boys themselves, (here Arthur Mee was not quite accurate. The Chapel belongs to the Chapel Trustees) and they set themselves the high purpose of carrying out the work without an architect and without paid labour. They found among them masons, plasterers, cement workers, carpenters, carvers of wood and stone, draughtsmen, sculptors and artists, and together they have overcome all difficulties, and acquitted themselves with his distinction."

Gorton left Blundell's in 1942 to take up his appointment as Bishop of Coventry. He was greatly loved by masters and pupils alike.

A memorial to the time of Gorton is the statue of the Welcoming Christ, carved by a pupil of Gorton, Allaine Johns, who was later killed in the War. There is a replica of this statue in the ruins of the old Cathedral at Coventry.

Most of Gorton's pupils would have seen war service soon after leaving school. Among such was Flight Lieutenant His Highness the Maharaja, Shrimant Yeskwantrao Jawhar (DB 1934-35).

During the second World War the O.T.C. was re-formed into the J.T.C. and Royal Naval and Royal Air Force sections were formed in 1942. To list those Old Blundellians who reached high rank and distinguished military service would be a very formidable task indeed, and even so, many great and brave men would be omitted through lack of careful research or plain ignorance. Men like Phillip Keun (F.H. 1926-29) who is referred to in Bruce Marshall's book about the French Resistance—*The White Rabbit*—under the code name "Captain Kane". Keun was awarded the Croix de Guerre and Legion d' honneur; he was murdered in Buchenwald concentration camp. Marshall records the memories of Wing Commander Yeo Thomas, G.C., M.C., as follows:

". . . The sixteen of them were to report to the Tower at once. At first neither the summoned nor their comrades were greatly alarmed, they thought that it was just some identity check . . . When the sixteen

27. Prof. A. V. Hill, C.H., O.B.E., F.R.S. (D.B. 1900-05, Governor 1919-44, President O.B. Club 1964-77). (From drawing by Edward I. Halliday).

28. Captain P. F. Grenier, R.N. (F.H. 1947-52) Commander of the new Destroyer H.M.S. Liverpool. (Press Association 12 May 1982).

29. Masters' Cricket XI in the late 1940's.
    l. to r. R. G. Seldon, P. L. Gillingham, A. R. B. Thomas, P. J. MacIlwaine, T. R. Jones, A. W. U. Robertson, J. W. S. Hardie, D. J. Rickards, S. H. Burton, G. W. Parker, W. H. Dowdeswell.

30. A group of F. H. boys in the 1940's.
    l. to r. O. H. D. Portsmouth, P. R. Broad, J. S. Read, Sir James Dalrymple-Hay, Bart., R. H. Champion, R. C. C. Thomas (later to become British Lions player and Capt. of Welsh Rugby XV).

failed to turn up for Appel in the evening, they still went on pretending that there was nothing wrong. That night, even although he had his bunk to himself, Yeo Thomas could not sleep. He had come to love Hubble and Kane as he had loved Brossolette. Were they too, to be taken from him? . . .

But in the morning after when Yeo Thomas again met his Polish friend in the small camp, the Pole stood to attention and saluted. 'I am sorry to have to tell you that your sixteen comrades were executed last night. There can be no doubt; one of our organisation has seen their bodies. They were brave men and we grieve for you.' The Pole then told Tommy of the manner of his friends' death; they had been hung by hooks in the wall of the crematorium and allowed to perish by slow strangulation; their corpses had been burned in the furnaces and the chimney had belched smoke all night. Tommy could not speak. For a few seconds he stood in silence. Then with tears in his eyes, he turned and walked back to his Block . . .''

After the war the Blundell's C.C.F., under the command of Major Grahame Parker, continued to wear the Devonshire regiment cap badge until 1959, when the defence costs under the Conservative Party resulted in the amalgamation of the Devons and Dorsets with the brigade cap badge. Although Blundell's retained very close contact with the Devons and Dorsets, the School adopted its own badge, the squirrel, which is still retained.

A cheerful letter from Sandhurst would be a regular feature in *The Blundellian*

February 1953

SANDHURST LETTER

Sir,

"Ship me somewhere east of Suez
Where the best is with the worst,
Where there 'aint no Ten Commandments,
And a man can raise a thirst.''

This thought constantly running through the minds of officer cadets at the R.M.A. will for seniors soon be a reality. We shall be leaving soon for that haven of irreproachable conduct, the officer's mess; from there many of us will use the world in much the same way as a bank clerk uses Cook's Travel Agency. The aridity of desert and the softness of sand, the neutrality of jungle and the bleakness of ice will soon open their uncompromising jaws to pip-conscious, pink faced young subalterns. No more for them the maniacal ravings of drill-drugged sergeant-majors. So it is with Derek Bendle and Colin Garland at the beginning of February. The former goes to join the Sappers while the latter has yet to find a regiment. Both have in their time here narrowly escaped becoming what for want of a better term may be described as the "D.S. officer cadet," in other words that most dreaded of military entities, the Sandhurst Type.

Michael Lamb wanders around with the careless "one-term-to-go-air" of the intermediate; he is generally to be found of a Saturday afternoon in the area of Deepcut . . . Tim Hume plays soccer. Enough said, Michael Martin plays company rugger with considerable energy, not a little skill and some success.

Michael Heath who is in Marne, is our only junior this term; he is just beginning to believe the assertion made by his elders that the modern C.S.M. is a past master at Ventriloquism.

Mons Company admitted three O.B. upstarts at the beginning of their current session. Cochrane Dyet can be observed leading the early morning rush to the Elephant and Castle for breakfast; he wears his beret with all the Pict ferocity of the Black Watch tam o'shanter. Burnand exercises our beagles in drain-pipe cavalry twills and a most impressive looking whip—always the picture of sartorial elegance, he is one of our leading fashion arbiters. Kilmister, meanwhile, works hard.

An interesting term so far, sir, enlivened among other events, by the visit of members of the R.N.C. Greenwich, to us on the night of November 5th; having daubed liberal brushes of white-wash over the front of the New Buildings and the Adjutant's car, they made off in the direction of Wokingham with one of our favourite cannons. The necessary reprisal, I regret to say, has yet to take place.

Yours, etc.,

SANDHURST.

The R.N. section was adopted by *H.M.S. Hermes,* and retained its tradition of doing everything at the double. Many OB., R.A.F. Officers would have made the initial step into the air via the Blundell's glider, or in latter years out of the air via the parachute dropping. Charlotte McKinnell made history by being the first Blundell's girl to volunteer for the parachute drop. She recalls that the School was either gallant or chauvinistic about it as they insisted that she had in addition to her parachute, a special automatically opening one. Boys were plentiful in the School at that time, girls were very rare. Bonnie Wilkens (G.H. 1977-

79) followed Charlotte's example, and now with over 280 free falls to her credit, she seems hooked on jumping out of planes; something her parents did not exactly plan when she was entered for the School.

Some of the old square bashing has now disappeared out of the corps—but a tie is now awarded to those who volunteer to go on Summer Corps Camp (in the old days they probably deserved a medal). The Colonel of the Devons and Dorsets visits the C.C.F. each year and the Corps has since 1974 used the Depot at Crickhowell as a base for Adventure Training. A party of 20 cadets visited the 1st Battalion for a week in Germany in 1978.

Sadly the mortality of Old Blundellians serving Officers did not come to an end at the close of World War II. The various peace-keeping roles and anti-terrorist activities that have since followed have taken their toll as shewn by the fresh memorial panels on the Chapel walls.

PRACTISING FOR BISLEY MEMBERS OF THE COMBINED CADET FORCE ON THE MINIATURE RANGE THE SCHOOL WON THE ASHBURTON SHIELD IN 1948, THE PUBLIC SCHOOLS SNAP SHOOTING IN 1948 AND 1953, AND THE GRAND AGGREGATE TROPHY IN 1952.
AFTER THREE AND A HALF CENTURIES: IMPRESSIONS OF BLUNDELL'S A GREAT ENGLISH PUBLIC SCHOOL.

The Illustrated London News Picture Library

16

Rev. Roger Lewis Roberts, C.V.O. (Headmaster 1943-47)

FOLLOWING Gorton in those tough war and post-war years, Roberts, although Headmaster for only four years, is remembered as an able administrator. The Blundell's of those years was still very much bare boards and cold baths compared to some of today's comforts. A thirteen or fourteen year-old might enter the School after being a monitor or prefect at his prep-school, yet now he would become the lowest of the low again—a fag. He would have little privacy, there would be a locker in his prep-room to keep his books in, and perhaps that photograph to remind him of home; that was allowed, although I can recall even in my time one junior desperately trying to convince a senior study, who had inspected his locker for tidiness, that the photograph of the lovely film star Anne Francis pinned on the inside of his locker door, was in fact a photo of his mother on the beach at Cannes, taken the previous summer. He would also have a games locker, similarly inspected for tidiness, and a 'tuck box' that would contain amongst other things, his shoe and corps-boot cleaning equipment, dubbin, blanco, etc. In the dormitory he would have a bed, a chair, and an open window.

The housemaster would invite the new boys to tea one Sunday, so also would a kindly house matron, (rather unfairly referred to as 'the Hag') carefully making sure that they were settled in. Sometimes the monitors would do likewise, for they, too, had once been new boys and understood what those first few days felt like. There would be two sorts of fag, the personal and the general. A personal fag was a kind of batman to a school or house monitor. He would have to keep his fagmaster's study tidy, cook certain meals for him, clean his rugger, cricket or corps kit and also run a few errands. Often two monitors would share the same study, so that the fags were able to work as a team—their reward: the privilege of being so-and-so's fag, plus ten shillings to one pound per term. Any familiarity was not encouraged at all, in fact it would have been viewed with acute suspicion by the other fags.

The general fag was given more specific house duties to do—cleaning the changing rooms, wash rooms and the 'bogs', as well as the other house common rooms and passages. Dustbins had to be carried to the end of the dog run on certain days and personal eggs and beans taken to the dining hall on behalf of the studies. Fag calls had to be answered and there were dining hall and dormitory duties as well. Strict standards were maintained. General fagging work was usually allocated by the head of prep-room, a boy usually in the third year, who would be answerable to the monitors for the smooth running of the prep-room.

Duties did not end after the official period of a fagging, usually a year. Second year prep-room also had specific house duties to perform, as did Junior studies, which included rota duties with the highly strung and temperamental house boiler and the mountains of coke that fed it. Senior studies would have to take it in turn to supervise prep and inspect the prep-room and changing rooms; there would also be corps responsibilities at this level, too. Was it not the great Dr. Arnold who said that boys should be governed as far as possible by the natural leaders among their own number?

A boy would be used to receiving and obeying orders, and also he would learn to give them and be responsible that they were carried out correctly. This was all part of the education and preparation for adult life. There was also a training in loyalty. Whatever boys might think of a certain monitor or senior study within their house, house loyalty would tend to prevent these feelings being passed on to boys of other houses, for when addressing them, your monitors were the best, your hag the nicest, and your House Master the most skilled in the use of the cane—for this some blood curdling and highly fictitious cases would be quoted—for if the truth be known, House Masters very rarely caned.

Occasionally there would be a break in protocol; for example there was a custom in some houses that once a term an event called 'The Prep-room Rag' was held. The head of house, being of a kindly and practical nature, would announce the event to the assembled house before evening prayers, to give them time for adequate preparation, both for this world and the next. Then about half an hour before the prep-room would be due for bed, the studies would raid the prep-room itself and there would be an almighty free-for-all. Like Jutland of old, victory would sometimes be claimed by both sides. On paper the studies obviously were more than a match for their Juniors, but it must be remembered that the Lower School were defending their own sacred territory, and often contingency plans would have been quickly put into operation, for example as to which particualr members of the Upper School they would concentrate on, tackling in groups hard and low. Thus, some bumptious senior study might suddenly find himself stuck under a pile of well organised fags with even a Junior study absentmindedly seated on his head—forgetting in the heat of the moment whose side he was on. They were generally good-natured affairs and did much to boost the morale of the youngsters, who in their dormitories, late into the night would gleefully recount some of the evening battles, such as how a group of them had managed to stuff old so-and-so into a dustbin whilst his mates were otherwise occupied.

A. R. B. Thomas recalled the boys in his 1975 OB. speech. ". . . The thing I most remember about them is their regard for the truth. Over and over again I have found boys who would not lie their way out of trouble, and this has inspired me a lot, so much so that when my monitors told me they suspected certain parties of law-breaking I told them the best thing was simply to ask them about it. But the monitors said 'No, that wouldn't be playing the game according to the accepted rules,' which were that people had to be caught in the act."

Monitors learned to temper justice with mercy; as on the occasion when a certain fag (I can't disclose from which house) decided to supplement his up to then mainly classical education with some practical Chemistry. The November firework night had not been a success and there were quite a number of dud fireworks. These he collected and having dried them out in the boiler house, proceeded to build a giant cannon out of their contents—as already stated, he had not yet started Chemistry. Placing his masterpiece by the coke heap at the back of the house, he lit the fuse and retired as per the printed instructions. If he had expected it to produce a fountain of colour, his expectations were eclipsed by what it actually did produce—thick, very thick, black smoke that kept continually pouring out of it, and, rising majestically upwards like a formidable storm cloud, it was wafted into the open dormitory windows by some passing zephyr. The house matron was in one such dormitory attending some malingerer . . . A posse of monitors was immediately summoned.

Two hours later the culprit, returning from a long walk, during which time he had hoped, in his youthful optimism that somehow matters would have cooled down, was met by a monitor at the house door. The housemaster had chosen his monitors wisely, and this was one of the best.

Perhaps he realised the hapless junior's vision of the remaining monitors drawing straws as to who was to thrash him, or of his headmaster composing a letter to his parents concerning his immediate removal, and although the monitor's own afternoon had probably been ruined by questioning likely culprits, his opening words disguised his personal inconvenience.

"The idea was great, that of gassing the Hag, but I'm afraid you slipped up on some of the finishing touches. She's still alive and creating stink."

The bewildered Junior did not think to deny the matter, but mumbled "How did you know it was me?" "Elimination, old chap. R.—would have done the job properly, H.—had a perfect alibi, B.—would not have wasted good smoke . . . etc" Then after giving the Junior a lecture on "If a job's worth doing . . ." he set him a nominal imposition and gave him a kind word of encouragement to continue his scientific investigations a little more discreetly.

Whatever important exams the Seniors would face, at no time could they use these pressures as an excuse to abdicate their responsibilities to the other boys. Yes, they obviously received certain privileges when they rose to the dizzy heights of school monitor, privileges that were highly envied by other seniors, but these privileges were just one side of the coin; the other side was authority coupled with heavy responsibility. They had come to the School as boys, they left as men.

Yet perhaps the supreme privilege given to a school monitor was that of being able to escort the partner of his choice to the Summer O.B. Dance at the School. They would emerge from their studies, resplendent in their evening dress (that tie so carefully knotted), and would stroll as unselfconsciously as they could in the magical evening light to the main buildings, proudly escorting some exquisite being from another world, who would be wearing one of those glorious evening gowns.

From the dark recesses of the houses, dozens of eyes would follow them, and boys, who by the end of that long, hard summer term had begun to seriously consider even their House Matron in a different light, were reassured that there were such things as girls after all. Perhaps a profound silence would be disturbed by someone 'in the know' (some enlightened government should severely tax experts and people 'in the know').

"You see the one in the turquoise dress with P.—?" All eyes would focus on that particualr enchanting creation, "She's R's sister!"

A gasp of disbelief and dismay would greet such an uncouth remark. Surely in no way could that lovely vision of an English rose, happily oblivious (or happily unobilivious) of the attention she was receiving, be related to that tick from N.C.

"Burton J. should be higher"
Feb 1962.

17

John Somers Carter, M.A. (Headmaster 1948-1959)

"Write a tribute to Carter—he was a great Headmaster". Request from two former Blundellians.

J. S. CARTER moved to Blundell's from St. John's, Leatherhead, where he had been a popular Headmaster. His time at Blundell's is remembered with respect and affection by many of his former pupils and staff. A very able scholar and administrator, Carter had a happy knack of getting the best out of people without visibly appearing to push them. His affectionate nickname amongst the boys was "Clueless Carter"—a misnomer as boys soon found out when they took on monitorial responsibilities, for behind the cheerful and rather vague mannerism he seemed to carry, was a very alert man who missed nothing; yet seemed to have an uncanny wisdom of when to act and when not to. A firm believer in the monitorial system, he chose his monitors very carefully and expected them to carry out their responsibilities fully and firmly, publically backing them to the hilt. Some of his outstanding Head-boys at Blundell's were Peter Watson (S.H. 1947-1952) a former Secretary of the Oxford University Rugby XV, Thomas Holden (W. 1949-1954) now a master at Eton, and Richard Sharp (W. 1952-1957), a former England Captain of Rugby. Two of Carter's former pupils at St. John's came to teach under him at Blundell's, M. E. C. ('Spike') Comer came in 1951 and Hugh Silk, ('Chips') former Head boy at St. John's, came in 1952.

A story is told about ten boys from Old House who had found a convenient cross-country route to a quiet pub on the outskirts of Tiverton, being more than mildly surprised one Sunday after Chapel to find their Headmaster quietly sitting in the lounge waiting for them. "Right, Gentlemen," he is reported to have said, "You may order your ten half pints now, drink up, and I will see you back in my study in an hour". In the Headmaster's Study each boy received the appropriate sharp six at the place where they were normally accustomed to sit down, along with the kindly warning that they should in future be more discreet about their drinking habits.

It was obvious that Carter both understood and liked his boys, they were very important to him, not just a necessary evil that went with the job. Motorists in a hurry down Blundell's Avenue were known more than once to have been flagged down by a gesticulating figure in a gown who would then politely explain in that clear voice of his that for his sins he happened to be the Headmaster of the School through which they were racing, and his responsibility for the safe keeping of the boys was being made more difficult by cars that were being impelled at great speed. He was not the sort of man who would either give or take offence, Humphrey Berkley records an amusing correspondence with Carter in the *Life and Death of H. Rochester Sneath*. Berkley, then an undergraduate at Cambridge, had invented a seemingly plausible but completely fictitious School which he named Selhurst; he even had notepaper printed "From the Headmaster of Selhurst, Petworth, Kent," and wrote long eccentric letters to the Headmasters of the leading Public Schools on subjects ranging from advice on rodent control, and laying of ghosts, to applying for the job of Master of Eton. Berkley managed to rile some of the Masters, but the good-natured Carter refused to take offence. Only the Masters of Winchester and Wimbledon actually spotted the hoax.

In 1954 Blundell's witnessed the happy occasion of its 350th anniversary when the preacher for the Thanksgiving Service was Dr. Fisher, Archbishop of Canterbury. The School was greatly honoured by the first of the visits of Her Majesty Queen Elizabeth, the Queen Mother, who attended on that occasion a sacred concert in the School Chapel given in her honour. Mr. Hall had produced a highly proficient Motet Club, a choir trained to a fine degree of excellence, and had even instilled a remarkable discipline in the remainder of the School's Chapel except for one notable case. It seems that Mr. Hall's acutely sensitive ears had been grossly offended for some time by one boy, who being completely tone deaf, was totally indiscriminate over the particular key in which he personally chose to sing, thereby shewing a remarkable degree of independence from the remainder of the School. As the entire School were undergoing the final rehearsal, Mr. Hall noticed, to his horror, that the place designated for the Queen Mother was directly in front of this particular *bête noir*. It has never really been satisfactorily proven as to whether Mr. Hall's subsequent action was motivated purely through his deep loyalty to the Crown or whether a desire for revenge had somehow crept in. Seizing this musical Philistine by the nearest convenient appendage, possibly an ear, he hauled him out of his seat and forced him to exchange places with another boy from the deepest recesses of the Chapel, and forbade him to return to his official seat until Her Majesty was safely back home in Windsor Castle. The boy who was denied his ringside seat had already suspected that he was possibly no latter day Caruso, so had in any case no intention of singing, for he too had a sincere respect for the Royal Family. The concert was an unqualified success, and the Queen Mother greatly endeared herself to the School, as she was to on subsequent occasions.

To find the strictest discipline within the School during any period, a keen student of history would have to look past the zenith of the monitorial system, past the C.C.F. being drilled by Quartermaster Davis, to the School Hospital. There, during the time of Carter, two loyal disciples of Florence Nighingale, Matron Smith and Sister Epps, carried an aura of discipline and efficiency that would have been the envy of the guards. Known affectionately as the 'Sanny Hags', these dedicated nurses commanded healthy respect from boys, masters and doctors alike. This Hospital was no place for malingerers or skivers trying to escape the Russell, or reluctant scholars attempting to avoid the consequences of failing to prepare a translation of Caesar's defeat of the Bellovaci (58 B.C.) for Mr. Clayton, first period Monday morning. These were the days when the nursing profession firmly believed in the value of purgatives. Many a Blundell's boy attending Hospital to have some limb, dislodged during a friendly game of rugger, returned to the position that the Creator originally intended it to be, or to have some embarrassing boil lanced, would at the same time have received the medical equivalent of an oil change when an innocent glass of grey liquid was given him to drink. These two ladies were totally loyal to the School, they loved the boys and would follow the careers of their former charges with interest and pride. Letters from old Blundellians were greatly treasured. When Colin Beale, the School Bursar, crashed through the ceiling whilst assisting Dr. Alec Camplin repair some faulty plumbing in the sanitorium roof, they were instantly able to recognise him from that half visible to them at the time and refused to have the area painted over afterwards—for that was now sacred.

Old Blundellians of Carter's time would still be in mid-career, but even so several have already distinguished themselves. Several who have entered the Forces have already reached high rank for their age, for example Lt. Col. Digby Willoughby, M.C. (W. 1948-1952) and Lt. Col.

John Beckingsale, M.B.E., M.C. (N.C. 1952-1957) and Capt. Peter Grenier, R.N. (F.H. 1948-1952). David Jewell, M.A. (P. 1947-1952) is currently Headmaster of Repton School. Anthony Lamb, M.A., D.T.A. (F.H. 1951-1956) is the Director of the large agricultural research station at Sabah, and was recently decorated by the King of Brunei. Lamb is also one of the world's leading authorities on orchids, and is the official orchid collector of Brunei. Peter Hurford (S.H. 1944-1948) who was a pupil under both Roberts and Carter is currently President of the Royal College of Organists.

18

Rev. John Maurice Stanton, M.A. (Headmaster 1959-1971)

THE Rev. Stanton presided over Blundell's during some exciting times of development, especially those achieved through the generosity of the Peter Blundell Society. The Peter Blundell Society was formed in 1951 during the time of Carter by an enlightened group of Old Blundellians, headed by T. Knox Shaw, the then Master of Sydney Sussex, deeply loyal to their old school, who faced up to the sad fact of life that heavy taxation on personal fortune made single generous benefactions such as Peter Blundell's, something very much of the past (though the School had also received generous gifts through John Coles and the Heathcote Amory family). These OB's felt it so important to demonstrate that an independent Public School such as Blundell's could remain truly independent, yet be willing and capable of not only looking after itself, but also provide the highest standards of education to meet the needs of the times, thus proving to be a valuable asset to the nation.

Many Old Blundellians and friends of the School therefore formally covenanted money or gifts through this newly formed society, the Peter Blundell Society, so that they could have a collective financial responsibility towards the future of their old School. By 1954 the P.B.S. was able to fund £15,000 for a badly needed new gymnasium and by 1956, £14,000 for important classroom extensions. In 1965, the School was honoured for the second time by the presence of Her Majesty Queen Elizabeth, the Queen Mother. This time she was to open a complex of beautifully designed new buildings which included a new Big School capable of seating over 500 people, a new Dining Hall and Kitchens, and a magnificent Music School complete with an orchestra practice room, thirteen practice rooms, two practice-cum-green rooms and extensive music storage space. The old Devonian Conglomerate stone quarries that had supplied the stone for the Victorian buildings had by then been worked out; the new buildings were therefore faced with artificial conglomerate, which when weathered would match the old. The consultant architect for this was Raglan Squire, F.R.I.B.A. (S.H. 1926-30), the son of Sir John Squire.

It was a great occasion and the Peter Blundell Society was able to proudly report back to its members:

"Visit of Her Majesty The Queen Mother.

"This was the second visit to Blundell's of Her Majesty Queen Elizabeth The Queen Mother. Her first visit was in 1954 on the occasion of the three hundred and fiftieth anniversary of our foundation. Her Majesty was therefore able to appreciate what has now been achieved.

"The day was a memorable one for the School and was the culmination of the first stage on the overall plan to which the Governors of the School and The Peter Blundell Society jointly had set their hands. We feel that Peter Blundell our founder—that robust example of the first Elizabethan era—would have enjoyed the day for here, following the example he had set, was evidence of vision and vigour and a firm faith in the future.

"On her arrival Her Majesty inspected the Guard of Honour and was then presented to the Governors of the School. She then formally opened the New Buildings with a silver key presented by the Head of the School. Thereafter Her Majesty unveiled the Plaque commemorating her visit and made a detailed tour of the Buildings and witnessed activities by the Boys of the School."

Standing in the crowd watching the events of the day was a former Prime Minister of Great Britain, Lord Home of the Hirsel. He was on a fishing holiday with two of the School Governors, the late Sir John Amory (who was then the Chairman of the Governors) and Sir John's younger brother, Viscount Amory of Tiverton, a former Chancellor of England and Governor of the School since he was 23 years old in 1923. Looking into the cheering assembly, the Queen Mother suddenly recognised Lord Home's face, and is reported to have exclaimed in a somewhat starled voice, "Alec, just where did you pop up from?"

Since that great occasion, the P.B.S. had continued to contribute to the needs of the School. The society has amongst other things arranged financial grants towards the cost of education at Blundell's, for the orphan son of any Old Blundellian, who would otherwise for financial reasons consequent on the death of his father be deprived of a Public School education, provided he passed the Entrance Examination in the normal way. In 1981 the Society launched an appeal to fund two major projects, part of the Governors' long-term development plans for the School. Firstly that of fundamental re-organisation and improvement of the School Science facilities and secondly, on the sports side, they aim to build one of the largest school sports halls in the country.

It was Stanton who thought one year that it would be a good experience for the boys to celebrate Easter for once at the School. It was a noble thought, though it meant also that the boys would be there on April the first. The morning of that particular date revealed that strange alterations had occurred in the night, white lines in the centre of the road swung through the School entrance taking traffic up to the tower where an effigy of the headmaster was found hanging from the top turret, field guns were strategically placed on the lawn, directed at the headmaster's study, whilst near Old Blundell's, ghostly footprints led from the statue of a certain royal personage to a local convenience and back. These sort of things would occur in any college rag but the *pièce de resistance* took place during the School Chapel practice. As was his wont, Mr. Hall wheeled his piano across to the centre aisle of the Chapel, preferring to direct the rehearsal of the Easter chants from there, rather than from the organ. Unknown to him, drawing pins had been stuck into each of the piano hammers. Winifred Atwell would have envied his magnificent opening notes for the Easter Anthem. It was quite a daring joke, as Hall was not usually a Master to trifle with. He took it well, perhaps those notes recalling for him what an earlier house once gave. How many of the schoolboys chuckling away there in the Chapel at that moment would have realised that Mr. Hall's nickname 'Jazz' was earned when, in his younger days at the end of the First World War, he had started his own jazz band? How many would have also realised in these days when a degree is awarded for every subject, is seems, except courtesy and manners, that Jazz Hall was in fact truly one of those gifted amateurs, completely self-taught in Music (his M.A. Oxon was for Classics), and that W. Lyons Wilson, that true artist, probably did not even know what the inside of an Art College looked like?

(The boys called him 'Jazz'; we Masters called him 'Sam'. I owe him a tremendous amount for his devotion to Music and especially the performances of Bach's Mass in B Minor. Nobody who sang in it can ever forget it. A.R.B.T.)

19

Arthur Clive Stanford Gimson, M.B.E., M.C., M.A.
(Headmaster 1971-1980)

IF A. L. Francis' historic decision to move the School from Old Blundell's to its present site in 1882 is considered to be one of the most fundamental and bold moves in the history of the School, surely it has a very close rival in the decision of Clive Gimson to include a limited number of girls into the sixth form in 1975, though he will be remembered for many other things as well, particularly his kind, sensitive nature. Initially only one girl was accepted, Arabella Ashworth, who came to Blundell's as its first girl, entering the sixth form in 1975. A. R. B. Thomas in his London OB. speech made some amusing observations;

". . . the coming of Arabella . . . heralding more of her kind . . . they will of course take over the School, . . . one of the Housemasters told me with some satisfaction that Arabella had already had a marked civilising effect on the boys. This was a new idea; so far as I could remember boys had been sent to School to become uncivilised and brutalised, hopefully ending up as barbarians. In this context I remember well the parting advice from the mother of a new boy as she left him behind at Francis House:- 'Well, you've a good Scots fist, and a good Scots tongue, so you'll be alright''. The boy in question has just finished managing and captaining the British Bobsleigh team in the Winter Olympics (Lt. Col. Ruari Cochrane-Dyet, F.H. 1947-1951). But I must confess I felt the first onslaught on civilisation a few years later when another mum left me with the direction that her son was to be given his pheno-barbitone regularly. Of course, he wasn't, but the writing was on the wall . . .''

Arabella Whitehead, (as she now is) has very kindly written her own reminiscences of her time at Blundell's.

31. 1956 Annual Inspection of Blundell's C.C.F. Major General R. W. Urquhart, C.B., D.S.O., Commandant of R.M.A. Sandhurst, talking to Major Grahame Parker, Commander of Blundell's C.C.F. (Photo *Tiverton Gazette*).

32. Her Majesty Queen Elizabeth, the Queen Mother Inspecting a Guard of Honour when she opened the new buildings 1967. (Photo *Tiverton Gazette*).

33. Francis House Play 1955 *Bats in the Belfry,* produced by Roger Cook, Geoffrey Hill and Nicholas Reynold.

34. North Close Play 1982 *Romanoff and Juliet.* Christopher Marjoram as Romanoff and Vicky Bertram as Juliet.

35. The 1967 buildings. Big School and Dining Hall. (Michael Huggins).

TWO POPULAR BLUNDELL'S WEDDINGS

36. Mr. A. R. B. Thomas to Miss Liddy Levo 1967. (Photo Gainsborough Studio).

37. Arabella Ashworth, Blundell's first VI form girl, and Ian Whitehead, fellow Blundellian, 1980 (Photo Peter Lowry).

BLUNDELL'S SCHOOL, TIVERTON, DEVON.

I joined Blundell's School in September, 1975 as the one and only girl amongst 400 boys. Needless to say, I was apprehensive!

I had been to Weirfield School in Taunton which had, within the last two years that I was there, amalgamated with the boy's Public School of Taunton. I was due to leave Weirfield in July, 1975 to go to Taunton, until the Blundell's Speech Day of that year. Both my younger brother who had previously been to St. Aubyn's School, (what is regarded as the Prep School to Blundell's) and my older brother who was in the process of taking Oxbridge were at Blundell's and my parents thought and still think that Blundell's is a good school especially as Piers, my elder brother, was doing so well and Carey's future looked promising. Piers, who had had to leave St. Paul's School, London was given the opportunity on arriving in the West Country of choosing the school that he liked most within a reasonable radius of Bridgwater where my father works and when he chose Blundell's, my parents then set about house hunting. So you can see just how much importance was attached to our schooling!

However, on that historical (in the eyes of the Ashworth family) Speech Day, it was announced that a decision had been arrived at to accept girls into Blundell's in the sixth form, in limited numbers (with a maximum of 25) and on a purely daily basis, i.e. no boarding because of lack of accommodation. When my parents came home to tell me what they had heard, I immediately wrote and asked for more details etc. I believe that such an immediate response was unexpected but I soon received an application form and later, the offer of an interview.

I remember the interview clearly as it was very casual and informal party because the Headmaster and the Milestones Housemaster, Mr. Wellesley were not used to dealing with girls! Soon after the initial interview, I was offered a place on the condition of attaining 5 'O' levels. I was warned that there might be only three or four of us, not expecting at that stage that I would be the only girl. I believe that two or three other girls applied for places but for some reason or other, they did not get accepted, or they turned down their places. I also think that preference was to be given to sisters of boys already at the school and this was an extra bonus on my behalf.

As I had taken up the offer of a place so quickly, no uniform or other arrangements had been made and Mrs. Gimson had to quickly create one and organise a study to be fitted in the top of the Headmasters house. I was to wear a dark grey skirt, a white shirt and a dark blue boys summer blazer. I was not very happy about the latter as the blazers were tailored to fit boys and not girls but I managed to get kitted out in time for the first day.

The most memorable occasion on the first day was chapel. I was taken in by one of the School Monitors and whenever I dared to raise my head, all I could see was a sea of staring, inquisitive eyes. So I spent most of that half hour staring at my hymn book!

I think that the boys were more afraid of me than I was of them as I was used to my two brothers and their friends. I was initially treated with great respect but as I became a familiar figure, this soon wore off! I spent a great deal of the first weeks on my own in my study where I used to retreat to get a little peace and quiet. Mrs. Gimson was very good to me especially in my first few weeks and I used to tell her how my day had gone and she would buck me up with a few cheering words.

I found it much easier to get on with the upper sixth form boys rather than the lower sixth, my own form, as the older boys were more mature and less childish so I did not get teased by them and therefore I found their company far more interesting. I used to be invited back to the boys studies and I must admit that the Housemasters were very trusting which gave me a lot of confidence and helped me to gain friends rather than being thought of as a threat to the smooth running of the boarding houses! I learned to like coffee by not liking to refuse an offer to go back to someone's study and thereby lose a possible friend but it took me a long time to be able to make a decent cup in return. In one way, having a study at the top of the Headmaster's house meant that I could not return these offers but it also meant that I had somewhere where I could get away from everyone if I so wished. I think that the freedom that I was given in the School was a very good way of letting the boys get to know me and to accept me as an equal rather than as a 'girl', or a threat to them or as somebody out of the ordinary as I was on my own.

During lessons, I did exactly as the boys and I was treated likewise, which led to that publicized comment about my wanting to be treated as one of the boys. This was the truth and I believe that I was not given preferential treatment in any way, except that I do know that I never had to write out 'sides'. Now, this may have been because I never warranted such a punishment (as I am, well certainly was, the sort of person not liking to break rules and being happy to conform) or because the Masters did not dare to make me do them! It was definitely noticeable that the boys in my classes were anxious to know how I was faring in the marking of essays and I think that my presence made them feel that they had to do well in order not to do worse than me—which was probably thought of as a great joke amongst one's friends if they couldn't keep up with the only girl in the school! I studied Geography, History and English and finished Blundell's with three 'A' levels, a General Paper and Use of English at a good enough level to qualify me for a University place. My results were not brilliant but satisfied me and my knowledge of my capabilities.

As I became better known, I used to spend more of my time in the day boy house of Milestones where I met my future husband when he was Head of House during his Oxbridge term. I used to share a study with three Upper Sixth form boys who, now I come to think of it, were all extremely tolerant of my invasion of their privacy. However, I did do some of the odd jobs in the study which paid for my keep, as it were! Any sewing that needed doing, especially rugger shorts which were indecent and the boys were due on the rugby pitch in 5 minutes, I undertook. It was also designated my job to apply the muscle cream before the matches much to my misfortune as I used to have piano lessons whilst the boys played sport and my long-suffering music master, Mr. Matthews, never knew that my playing was affected by my red-hot finger tips which was a result of this particular preparation. I think if he knew that I had been massaging the boys shoulders, I should have been banned from the House altogether!

I played hockey whilst I was at Blundell's, much to everyone's amusement and one of my habits was to go into the boys changing rooms already changed myself and assuming, in all innocence, that they would be ready too. All activity would stop when I went in and there would be much tidying of lockers until somebody plucked up the courage to tell me that they would be ready in 5 minutes if I would care to wait outside?! I also used to use the mirror in their changing room when I thought nobody was about, and I have had to make many rapid exits to save my face and that of the occupants, though they never knew that I was there. When I was in one of the boarding houses one afternoon, visiting a friend, I came down the stairs at the bottom of which was the door to the changing room. On this particular occasion, as I reached the top of the step, the door was flung open and a young boy of about 15 stood there totally naked, and obviously the last thing he expected to see was me. There was an almighty yell, followed by several unmentionable expletives and a great deal of laughter. Now, being short-sighted and at that time, not wanting to wear glasses (I now wear contact-lenses), the impact was lost on me but this made no difference to the boy in question and he suffered a great deal of tormenting from his friends for some time afterwards!

One example of how I wanted to be accepted as an integral part of the school occurred when on a Geography Field Trip to the Malvern Hills. When we arrived at the centre where we were to be staying during the five days that we were in the area, all the boys were given adjacent rooms while I was give a little flatlet on my own, quite a way from everyone else. I put my foot down at this, went straight into the corridor of the adjoining rooms, plonked my bags in a room and stayed there, whilst an unfortunate latecomer had to put up with the flatlet!

When I first arrived at Blundell's, fresh from my all girls school I noticed several differences. Though discipline was still enforced, it did not take such importance and was more of an accepted norm than a terrible punishment. A detention in a girls school seemed to carry far more weight to the girls than similar punishment at Blundell's. The atmosphere in the classroom seemed far more relaxed and total silence was not necessary. This change may have been because I had entered a sixth form and was comparing it with my fifth form at Weirfield but at the time, it made me feel that boys schools were obviously far more fun and I regretted what I had been missing up to that time.

When I was joined in my second year by five new girls, I was starting to settle down to hard work in preparation for my 'A' levels, and I concentrated more on study than on play. I also had a permanent boyfriend (my husband) so life was more settled and school was no longer a novelty.

Blundell's gave me a great deal and I shall always look back on my year as the only girl with great pleasure as my memories are only happy ones. Recently, I went to a job interview where I was quizzed on my schools and it was suggested that because I had been to Public School, that I had experienced a very sheltered upbringing. I immediately disputed this as I feel that I have more to offer having been to Blundell's, having coped with a year on my own in a boys school and that Public School does not shelter one from the outside world as many people seem to think provided all the opportunities that are offered one whilst at school are taken up and used to your best possible advantage.

Blundell's gave me great confidence in myself, (though I don't think that I was particularly unsure of myself before I went there, as I have travelled fairly widely and I had already come from a Private School), and also a good start in life. No matter what people say or think, the fact that one has been to Public School still holds for quite a lot, the same as saying that one has been to either Oxford or Cambridge, and it is recognised as something worthwhile rather than as a disadvantage. I feel that whatever anyone says, it cannot be taken away from you that you have had a Public School education and more often than not, this fact goes in your favour rather than against it.

One thing that shows how much I value having been to Blundell's and a view that is also shared by my husband, is that if we have children and we can possibly affort it, it is the sort of schooling that we would choose, though by the time we shall be thinking of such matters, such a choice will probably have been taken away from us. I believe that it is possible to receive a good schooling from the State system but one does not necessarily receive the other things that creates a mature and whole person.

Blundell's School has certainly given me a great deal, also my husband and my two brothers and none of us has ever regretted having had a Public School education. I am pleased that the subsequent female pupils at the school are doing so well—I believe that the taking of girls at sixth form level can only benefit the school providing that they add to and don't detract from the school. I know that it is a break in tradition but I think that it is for the best ends and if it gives the school a boost, then it has been worthwhile.

From a candidate's answer:

"A considerable number of La Fontaine's fables were really written by Aesop."

20

Sport at Blundell's

"Blundell's are our Dearest Foes". (Rudyard Kipling, *Stalky & Co.*)

Rugby Football

Whether it was Jack Russell with his pack of hounds in the early 1800's or the formidable senior Russell cross-country course of this century, sport has come readily to a school surrounded by such rich Devonshire countryside, and football (rugger), has always held the premier colour.

Like many other schools Blundell's had developed its own style of football by the early part of the nineteenth century, and it would be most interesting now to witness a game played to those ancient rules. Lewis Wells (OB 1858-1860) was the first to introduce the drop-kick in this School at a time when punting was in fashion, and alter the game from kicking and dribbling to a modified style of Rugby football. Rugby football rules were introduced in 1868 replacing the "peculiar and extraordinary code of Blundell's rules." It is interesting to note that Dr. Frederick Temple was at that time Headmaster of Rugby. He had been a very keen footballer when he was at Blundell's and he had done much to reform games at Rugby. Dr. Salter, recollecting Temple to the Rev. J. C. Hughes, said the following: "He was a good football player . . . I have a vivid recollection of the activity he displayed, rushing to and fro with trousers much too short, coarse blue worsted stockings and big heavy shoes. Woe to the player with whom those shoes came into contact! But the wearer was not spared in return." Temple himself recollected; "In 1833 when I came football was at its height, and on the second day I was drawn for a match and told by a big boy to stand at the goal and not let the ball past. Soon afterwards the ball came that way, and I rushed towards it, but before I could think of the consequences, I was kicked with the ball right through the goal. After that I was looked upon as a courageous football player, and to this day I have on my shins the marks of the kicks received at that game." When Temple left the School, he was proclaimed the best-footballer there.

The boys at Blundell's obviously preferred the Rugby rules, as letters in the Blundellian of that period indicated. One OB summed the matter up. "I am quite sure that the Rugby game is far superior to the old school game, and even if that were not the case, the Rugby rules are so universally played throughout the whole of England that the fact of having been accustomed to another game places the Blundellian under a great disadvantage after he has left the School."

E. R. Crowe in his "A hundred years of rugger at Blundell's", gives an interesting insight into the "field and green" tradition by reproducing a clipping from the Tiverton Gazette of 22nd November, 1870 on the match between Blundell's and Newton College. "There was a little pitch at first as the Newtonians, when they saw Blundell's time-honoured yard positively refused to risk their persons in it, but thanks to the generosity of Mr. Glendinning and the Cricket Club, this deficiency was supplied and the result was a highly contented game, neither side being able to gain a goal, though Blundellians, under the disadvantages of strange rules and a roomier ground than usual, were the harder pressed of the two."

The old green was proving too small for the Rugby rules, so the School gained permission to use the Tiverton Athletic field for the first game, and the second game was played on the green. The top game is still called "the Field" and the second game "the Green". (The third game used to be called "the Block", because it used to be played near the old flogging block).

Blundell's soon developed a particularly tough style of Rugger, so much so that in the *Blundellian* of 1878, regretting the number of football accidents which compelled boys to stay away from School from time to time, pointed out that "football is one of the best things in the world but must not elbow education out of the way . . .". The "Blundellian" expected good tough players and the First XV write-ups could be very blunt.

1890. F. R. Bingham—A fair heavy-weight forward, rather too gentle with his opponents; wants judgements in a crisis.

1894. S. J. C. Clarke—Always plays fully up to his weight and strength, has set a good example in not letting his collaring and charging become feeble through over politeness.

. . . has set a good example in not letting his collaring and charging become feeble through our politeness.

1894. C. H. Harper—Undoubtedly the best forward in the XV. In every match has played a strong and sound game from kick-off to finish.

(C. H. Harper (O.H. 1889-1895) went on to captain Oxford University XV in 1898 and to play for England in 1899. He was to become the Governor of the island of St. Helena).

1895. A. O. Parker—has been lucky in retaining his place, too sleepy to deserve it.

In the "Blundellian" of December, 1895, it was pointed out that "All injuries on the football field are not to be remedied by laying the sufferer on his back, pulling out his legs and applying a system of massage indiscriminately. We know a case of a broken ankle, where well-meaning members of the team sat on the wounded foot and adopted the treatment recommended for restoring life to the half-drowned." But the spirit of the game was infectious and it was difficult for some bystanders to stand idly by:

"To the Editor of the 'Blundellian', 1896.

Sir,
    Is it in the power of the Football Captain of the Games Committee, or the Chief Superintendent of Police to devize means whereby dogs may be kept off the field of play during the progress of a match? Against Taunton an irresponsible black puppy entered so thoroughly into the spirit of the game that he once looked like scoring a try on his own account. Things were even worse at the Newton match. No less than three dogs cut in, so to say; one of them quite capable of winning the game for his side. . . ."

For past and present Blundellians wishing to delve into the rich history of Blundell's rugger we would warmly recommend E. R. Crowe's book "A Hundred Years of Rugger at Blundell's." Suffice to say that the Blundell's crest hangs along with those of the oldest playing Clubs and Schools in the main room at Twickenham.

Like most good Schools, Blundell's has had its vintage years, such as in 1878 and 1899. For example, in 1899 no School opponents were able to score any points against Blundell's 246; or in 1940 when in their first year of entry Blundell's, captained by W. J. Hotblack (W. 1935-1940) captured the Public Schools sevens at Richmond beating Dulwich in a memorable final 28-0, where each of the Blundell's players scored. Forty-one years later in 1981 Blundell's beat the much fancied Monmouth side, three times winners of the Festival, 16-8 in the final of the Rosslyn Park National Schools Sevens at Roehampton.

There have been amusing incidents, times when young masters even managed to slip into the School XV, or as in 1926, under T. R. K. Jones ('Jonah'), Masters were able to play together and help to defeat a hitherto unbeaten School side, Jonah was awarded a Cambridge blue as a back row forward and had the unusual distinction of getting trials for both Wales and England. As A. R. B. Thomas recalls in his O.B. speech.

    . . . Eighty or nintey years ago masters played in the School teams, and even 50 years ago, they occasionally played in The Field. I well remember Herb Batterbee playing in The Field when he was 42. I remember Wansbrough French playing on the right wing and sending over the cross-kick from which Jonah was bound to score. In 1926 the

School had a pretty good team, beating Seale Hayne 63-0, R.N.C. Dartmouth 16-3, Sherborne 16-3, Exeter Club 1st XV 9-6, and Clifton Club 16-0. It was captained by C. L. (Cow) Ashford, who later got his Blue at Cambridge and obtained fame in the legal world. But his XV was beaten by a very strong side that Jonah brought along, and I mention this because three of that victorious team are here tonight—Ronald (Ronald Seldon, Master 1926-1964) was the fly-half and converted five of the tries: I was full-back and didn't have much to do, and Ben Lewin was in the pack (Wilfred Roy Lewin, Master 1926-36). Four of us played regularly for Tiverton, Ronald and Bill Thoseby, S. E. Wilson and myself. I pair them like that because that's how they were paired in the days of Dark and Light Blue. So far as I was concerned the feature of these games was the crowd (on whatever Devon ground one played). It was utterly partisan, it lusted for blood, and it scared the life out of the referee; it could have been similar to the crowds that filled the Coliseum in the days of Ancient Rome. A roar of approval broke out when boots and fists went flying in a maul; a united shout of "Offside Ref" went up whenever the opposition looked like scoring, and a throaty and unearthly crackle went round the ground whenever the referee gave in and blew his whistle, thus stopping a perfectly legal try."

There was also the time when Cranleigh unwittingly fielded 16 men—against Blundell's 14; solemnly reported in the "Sportsman" of December, 23rd 1921. The School XV was unbeaten in 1936 and 1937 and there were some really outstanding XV's in the 1950's and 1960's. The future looked bright, the Newtes—the most junior side having produced scores of over 40-0 twice and 80-0 once in the 1980 season,—obviously trying to emulate the Blundell's XV of 1899 which defeated a shattered Newton College 146-0 on November, 17th 1900. In 1982 the School won the Devon Schools under 15 rugby final, beating Hele 23-3.

During the last hundred years Blundell's have produced a steady stream of English, Irish, Welsh and even Australian caps along with a liberal sprinkling of Oxford and Cambridge Blues. The first recorded international from Blundell's was R. S. Kindersley who played for Oxford 1882, 1883 and England 1883-1885. Outstanding within this group of internationals were T. S. Kelly who gained 12 English caps, and Captained England, 1908 (D.B 1895-1898), R. C. C. Thomas (F.H. 1942-47) who was capped 26 times for Wales and also R. A. W. Sharp (W. 1952-1957) capped 14 times for England, both Thomas and Sharp having been on British Lions tours. Sharp went on to teach at Sherborne, including the coaching of their teams at Rugger. Sherborne who had always given Blundell's a tough game, certainly didn't need encouraging any more.

Charles P. Kent (N.C. 1966-1971) has had several seasons playing for England. He was Captain of Oxford University Rugby Club 1974-1975.

Reflecting on the records, it would be fair to say that inter-house matches have always been keenly and evenly fought, and each house contributed well to the School XV. As A. R. B. Thomas has already pointed out, however, "the speed School House fags answered fag whistles around the right-angled bends of the house corridors helped maintain that particular houses tradition of jinking three quarters and fly halves".

There have been other theories, "The best halves we have ever had, Dakeyne and Stevens, got their nimbleness from the gymnasium" (from *The Blundellian* of 1895).

Cricket

Cricket seems to have been played at Blundell's by the nineteenth century, one of the earliest recorded cricket coaches was Parson Pole, who, when at Oxford, played in the first match against Cambridge in 1827. Temple enjoyed cricket as a pupil at Blundell's in the 1830's, and his first words as the newly-appointed Headmaster of Rugby to the Captain of cricket there were, "Well, Sandford, how's the cricket". He even played cricket as Archbishop of Canterbury with the American Bishops on his lawns at Fulham and beat them soundly. During his last visit to the School as Archbishop of Canterbury he was seen wandering about the Old Green beset by a swarm of youngsters, showing them among other things the spot where he had received a bad blow in the eye from a cricket ball. The atmosphere of these early cricket matches had been captured in the memoirs of one Old Blundellian, who paints an interesting picture of cricket at the Old School in the 1840's: "The green . . . was divided into two parts by the causeway. The part on the right to one entering through the gateway was devoted to cricket, that on the left to football. The boys did all the work for the cricket ground except for mowing. We picked up the broken bits of lime branches and rolled it diligently, and kept it in good order. The ground was absurdly small, but we enjoyed our games, and hit as hard against the trees and walls as if we had plenty of room, and some of us learned to distinguish ourselves in after years."

The first recognised School XI seems to be in about 1859, when the School played Calver Vale, The Rev. C. Beres XI and Tiverton. Through the years there have been the great cricket names such as C. T. A.

Wilkinson, who played regularly for Surrey and captained the County when they won the championship in 1914 and also in 1919 and 1920, S. G. U. Considine (W. 1915-1919) who played cricket for Somerset, (and Rugby for England) in the 1920's, E. T. Benson who toured New Zealand with the M.C.C. in 1929-1930 tour, and Roger C. Davis (F.H. 1959-1964) who played regularly for Glamorgan, including the side that won the 1969 County Championship. In 1969 G. I. R. Harvey (O.H. 1955-59) won the Wilfred Rhodes Trophy awarded to the outstanding player in minor county cricket. Currently Vic Marks (F.H. 1968-1973 and Master 1978-1981) and Jeremy Lloyds (F.H. 1968-1973) play for Somerset, and Vic played for England in 1980 and 1982.

Through the years, old editions of *The Blundellian* give insight to the first XI characters of yesteryear,

July 1919   S. G. U. Considine. His century against Sherborne is an innings not to be forgotten. Times the ball better than ever. Has all his old shots with some dangerous additions. Playing back does not always cover the ball going away. He must learn to leave alone the tempting good length ball on the off and to play himself in with more patience. Smart and reliable as a wicket-keeper.

(Considine played for Somerset whilst still at School and also played for the 'Rest' in the school Test match at Lord's in 1919, making 118, the highest score in the game).

July 1922   K. H. Baines (Capt.). A forcing batsman with many good strokes through the covers and on the on side; inclined to undercut towards point; his century against the Town was a splendid piece of work. As Captain he has managed some variable bowling with very good judgement and placed his field well. His personal keenness and knowledgable interest on the points of the game have been undoubted factors in the season's success. An improved field, but inclined to stand too far in at mid-off.

July 1930   P. H. Seymour. A good cricketer who did not find his form or confidence until this season. Has a good defence and watches the ball carefully. Is inclined to follow the leg ball round to fine leg instead of playing it to mid-on. Has good scoring strokes on the off-side, chiefly behind the wicket. A close fielder and a good catch. (The Hon. P. H. Seymour is now the Duke of Somerset.)

1946   E. R. Crowe—a brilliant fielder, probably the best for years at silly point especially, where he swallowed catch after catch—highest innings 77. (The name E. R. Crowe, M.A. (F.H. 1943-1946) heads the list of assistant Masters at the School in 1982.)

Sept. 1950   H. R. Bayly. Improved considerably as a batsman through the term. Started shakily with a lack of confidence which affected his footwork. Played several neat and effective innings, distinguished chiefly by good strokes past mid-on. Keen and alert fielder.

(Hugh Bayly captained the Francis House Cricket team that toured Holland in 1949. This team was the first English side ever to play on the Quick cricket ground. Hugh Bayly also had an Olympic trial for skiing in the 1950's and is currently the school registrar).

1981   Hugh Morris scored 923 runs (averaging 184.6) and captained the England Under 19's side. He scored two centuries for Glamorgan 2nd and played his first county game against Leicestershire and faced Andy Roberts, one of the most feared fast bowlers in the world.

An account of Blundell's cricket would no be complete without a reference to Tom Jennings a Cricket professional and head groundsman 1924-1962. He played many times for Devon and became a county umpire. He came to Blundell's from a Surrey career as a left arm bowler.

Shooting

To have captured the Ashburton trophy at Bisley, that coveted Public School prize, must be the hallmark of any vintage year. The Blundell's Eight have returned twice in triumph with this most coveted trophy; in 1946 under Mr. Abigail and in 1956 under Lt. W. R. Brooke-Smith, R.N. The triumphant VIII at Bisley in 1956 did not just return with the Ashburton, but also they brought back to keep it company the grand aggregate trophy (with a record score) and the Marling (out of the 40 shots, 26 bulls, 14 inners, no magpies, no outers, no misses). The School was just pipped into second place for the Snap and Rapid. That year Blundell's also captured the Devon Open County Astor and were unbeaten by any other school, including Allhallows.

The 1956 successes were really the climax of several outstanding shooting VIII's of that period, and much of the success would surely be due to the extremely high degree of coaching given by the School Quartermaster, that very distinguished soldier, Lt. Stan Davis, ex Grenadier Guards, ex Burma Railway. To start with, Davis was an outstanding gunsmith. No boy was ever allowed to represent the School without his No. 4 Lee-Enfield being in 100% condition. Every year Davis would thoroughly strip down and re-bed each rifle. He would also spend infinite care ensuring that every member of the shooting cadre could achieve the ideal shooting position like a second nature. Snapping practice was compulsory at least twice a week on the cinder track, and trigger pulling and flinching was soon eliminated by the strategic use of a penny (1d.!) across the foresight guard.

In 1953 the Honourable Artillery Company gave Blundell's the privilege, along with Uppingham, Allhallows, Cheltenham, Wellington and Sherborne, of leaving the tent lines and using the H.A.C. Club House instead as their dormitory.

Old Blundellians' shooting re-unions continue via the Blundell's Magpies Rifle Club. Ben Wrey (W. 1953-1958) three times a Cambridge blue and Queen's prize finalist eleven times, has represented England and Great Britain many times. David Bentata (F.H. 1951-1956), an Oxford Shooting blue, represented the joint Oxford and Cambridge rifle teams in the 1961 East African tour—during which he was seconded to stalk a rogue elephant, which he killed with the first shot. Bentata still shoots and coaches with the Oxford and Cambridge Rifle Association, as well as being, with Ben Wrey, the official Bisley coach to the Blundell's Magpie Rifle Club. Since 1973 the School has won the First Division of the British Schools Rifle Association 'B' Group, service .22, twenty times and has now won the British Schools VIII two years in a row with a new record score, having only dropped 21 points out of 2,400. The School 'B' team was fourth in the same competition.

Athletics

Athletics used to be regarded by some as a convalescent period that followed the Junior, Inter and Senior Russells, those formidable and compulsory cross-country runs that absorb the first half of the Easter term, the details of which would be found only in the very small print of a prospectus. Traditionally athletics seemed to have developed from those early May 29th celebrations, and included in the early days jumping for "treaklers" and a form of apple bobbing that seemed to include a liberal amount of treacle and feathers in the proceedings. The mile was six times around the old green, but it did tend, it appears, to be a bit of an obstacle race as runners had to dodge some of the branches and roots of the old limes in the process. The hundred yards required a living barrier against the School House walls to act as a human brake for the runners. Throwing the cricket ball, diagonally across the green, required careful use of Euclid to calculate the distance if a certain lime tree had not impeded the flight of the ball. Putting the Shot (here the ironing box was used) and Throwing the Hammer sounded positively dangerous, especially as the shot was put from the base towards the apex of the ironing box, yet there do not appear to be any recorded cases of a spectator being actually brained in the process.

When the School moved to the Horsdon site with its spacious playing fields, much of the more 'rural' aspect of sports disappeared including "jingling" and the more serious recording of athletic results developed. The pride of Blundell's athletics must go to the one time President of the Cambridge University Club J. W. J. Rinkel (W. 1920-1924) who ran the quarter mile for England in the Olympic Games, and J. P. Thornicroft (N.C. 1934-1939) who held the Public Schools 440 yards record for many years. Rinkel got the only double when he represented the English at Harvard in 1926 in the 220 and 440, against Harvard and Yale, winning both races. Also C. H. Stoneley (F.H. 1926-1930) represented England in the Olympics.

Cross-Country Running

The cross-country steeple-chase called the Russell was of nineteenth century foundation before the School moved to Horsden. Started in 1877 it is named after that colourful Old Blundellian, Parson Jack Russell, who was all for steeple-chasing, providing in his case he was seated astride a horse. The early races were often started by the sounding of a hunting horn. The Russell became a team race in 1919. There are three main courses now, the Junior, the Intermediate and the Open, which is supposed to be only 5½ miles, though they must be Devonshire miles. Traditionally, unless a pupil was either certified dead or legless, these runs were compulsory; there were not even religious grounds available for dissent. One former Blundell's Master, on reading our script, has kindly pointed out that we are perhaps forgetting that medicals were available before the Russell was run. If a boy was obviously a good runner he was sent to Dr. Lowe, who thoroughly examined the boy and made him run the Russell in any case; but if the boy was an indifferent runner and there seemed a possibility that his complaint was genuine, he would then be sent to Dr. Graham, who had been known to show compassion in such cases.

There was once a farmer near the School who prided himself on his ridge and farrow ploughing in the days when ridges were narrow and set high. The course often seemed to fall along the ridges rather than across them. The Lowman river through which the course winds backwards and forwards is not a heated swimming pool in February. It is because of this that farmers who are Old Blundellians are easily recognised as such, by the careful and sympathetic manner in which they dip their sheep.

Peter Grenier (F.H. 1948-1952), had a system of punishment that, had it been adopted universally in the schools throughout the country, would have saved this country millions of pounds in Remand Centres, Probation Officers, Social Workers and sundry assorted phychiatrists. Dispensing with his monitorial right to use the cane, or set sides in English, Latin or Greek, or dish out House duties, he merely ordered that the offenders accompany him on one of his early morning training runs. The Eton flogging stool pales into insignificance at this. A. R. B. Thomas recalls the happy event of Grenier, with one or two friends, requesting permission to do a training run to Bampton Fair and back. Mr. Thomas decided to motor out to see how they had faired, and stopping at an Inn on the way asked some local men if they had seen the cross-country runners. The men obviously had showed an interest, and affirming that they had, added "and the chestnut was the in lead".

D. A. Rickards, (Master 1934-1953), came to Blundell's with a fine athletic record from Sedbergh and Cambridge, winner of his School 10 mile cross-country race, as already mentioned. Rickards was still running the Blundell's Senior Russell course himself at the age of 40, a month before he left to become the first Headmaster of Welbeck. Charlotte McKinnel, one of the first sixth-form girls at Blundell's, commanded a healthy respect from the rest of the School by volunteering not only to run in the Junior Russell of 1977, but managing to come in the first 50, thereby obtaining a House point.

Fives

The earliest sport recorded at Blundell's seems to be fives. Dunsford writes that in 1699 the Summer Assizes was held at Mr. Blundell's School, in Tiverton. The Judges names were, the Lord Chief Baron Wild, and Mr. Justice Rigby: the former sat in the fives place in the School House green; and the latter at the desk of the Higher School. The playing of fives against the School walls may be the possible clue that H. R. Viles was searching for when in his 1974 Mahood Prize Essay on the School account between 1670-1679, he made this observation: "Indeed glazing work was regular and frequent. In April 1670 a bill from Will Chilcott came to £15. 17s."

38. The Bisley Team 1956. (Photo Gale & Polden Ltd.).

Standing: Mr. Brooke Smith   A. P. Wright   C. B. Bradford   W. D. Thomas   A. R. Mundy   Lt. A. S. Davis, O.B.E.
Sitting: D. W. Willoughby   M. D. A. Bentata   P. M. Jones   J. M. Palmer (Capt.)   K. M. T. Maddock (Sec.)   B. M. B. Wrey
J. A. Batten   T. K. Courtenay

39. A strong F.H. Cricket XI 1950. Captained by Hugh Bayly, present Registrar. (Photo Chandler).

Back row l. to r.: P. F. Grenier, C. W. M. Grose, P. R. Ash, N. A. Clatworthy, D. G. Petrie, J. D. Jowitt.
Front row l. to r.: R. Dalrymple-Hay, J. D. W. Maclean, H. R. Bayly, G. L. Lang, C. S. Hilliard.

40. The First XI 1955. (Photo Chandler)

D. V. Tayor,   T. F. A. Thomas,   C. J. A. Clarke,   A. J. N. Edwards,   C. Mumford,   J. J. G. Edwards,   T. Jennings
A. R. Tinniswood,   R. J. Firth,   J. J. M. Street (Capt.),   R. A. W. Sharp,   F. J. Davis

41. The First XI 1981.

Standing: Mr. E. D. Fursdon, M. G. Beard, G. M. Dee Shapland, C. E. Faye, J. M. D. McKinnel, J. W. H. Trafford, R. J. Taverner, A. G. Craze, Mr. E. Steele.
Seated: P. S. Selley, P. D. Langdon, H. Morris, S. A. Watts, R. A. Eustace.

When the buttresses were built against the front of the School the Foeffees in 1841 decided to spend not more than £20 in making a fives court in the south-eastern angle of the green, as the type of fives that is still played at the School are the Rugby fives.

In 1923, when Eton pipped Blundell's into second place in a magnificently fought contest for the Ashburton Shield at Bisley, the Master of Eton sent this message to Blundell's.

"I hear that at Blundell's they are building some new Fives courts; now if they are sensible and build ETON courts, they can have their revenge any day they like."

The new RUGBY Fives courts were opened in 1924, and incidentally, Blundell's chose a different field of sport to get some revenge on Eton—at the 1929 OTC Camp at Tidworth, the Blundell's contingent won an outstanding victory over a heavier Eton team in the Tug-of-war final. In 1959 C. J. McLachlan and R. W. White won the Public Schools Open Doubles Championships.

A respectable year for fives could be, for example, 1972;

1st IV	v. Sherborne	(H) won 180-59
	v. Colston's	(A) won 165-73
	v. Clifton	(H) won 180-46
	v 'Jokers'	(H) won 180-52
	v Jesters	(H) won 157-124
	v Exeter University	(A) won 118-114
	v Bristol G.S.	(A) won 169-51
	v Old Blundellians	(H) won 164-97

1st IV C. E. M. Colquhoun, V. J. Marks, A. Beddoe, S. J. Wright.

V. J. Marks became an Oxford Fives Blue, and also captained the Oxford University Cricket Club in 1976 and 1977.

Other Sports

In 1730 the Feoffees ordered that all cockfighting at the School House on Shrove Tuesdays be abolished for the future. (In 1763 Henry Hingeston, a Quaker at Kingsbridge, classed cockfighting along with footballers and the wrecking of ships.)

Rowing is not a sport associated with this School, yet Blundell's boys used to claim the right when the Exe or Lowman flooded, to break open the brewery next door and use the tubs as punts. Dunsford records

Blundell's boys rowing about in tubs in the December 1695 floods, and those of 12th October 1753, and Snell records the same thing happening in 1865.

During the latter part of the nineteenth century, gymnastics were capped, and the Public Schools annual Gymnastics and Boxing Competitions at Aldershot held in March became an important event. The Golf Club was also taken very seriously. D. I. Stirk (F.H. 1930-34) was London University Champion in 1939, and Devon Open Champion in 1964 and 1972. In the past, half colours have been awarded for fives, boxing, fencing, tennis and swimming. In very recent years Association Football and hockey have also been reintroduced as half colour sports, and squash and judo are also listed. In 1920, C. T. A. Wilkinson won a Gold Medal for Britain in the Olympics, at Hockey.

In 1974 the School team won the National Schools Show Jumping Championships at Hickstead.

Full Colours

Sports colours have always been hard won, especially full colours. One of the all-time outstanding all rounders must have been J. J. M. Street (W. 1950-1956) who obtained four full colours, Rugby, Cricket, Athletics and Cross Country as well as a fencing half colour. (The only other possible full colour available at that time was for shooting). Street was, incidentally, also Head of School, Captain of Rugby and Captain of Cricket. He captained the 1956 Blundell's Rugby side that defeated their arch rivals Sherborne 33-3. This was one of those periods of extremely stiff sports competition, with sportsmen like Richard Sharp (W. 1952-1957), himself a triple colour, Richard Hein (F.H. 1950-1954), a double full colour, whose cricket centuries seemed to become a regular feature in sports columns of the *Western Morning News* and *Daily Telegraph*, Christopher Higgins (M. 1951-1957), Nicholas Bourne (P. 1952-1957), John Beckingsale (N.C. 1952-1957) and many others including a select group of the inevitable Welsh Rugger contingent with names like Terence Thomas (S.H. 1952-1956) F. J. Davis (F.H. 1952-1957) and M. M. Davies (F.H. 1953-1957).

And the Ladies

The recent admission of a limited number of sixth-form girls into the School, has resulted in fresh traditions developing in the world of sport. Ignoring any temptation to enforce women's lib. on the Field or the Green, these spirited young ladies have already produced some excellent hockey XI's and also built up a formidable fencing tradition by winning the under 19 Devon Ladies Fencing Championships three years in a row.

>1978—Charlotte McKinnel (who incidentally was the first girl to represent Blundell's at a sport and also to receive a half colour.)
>
>1979—Rachel Jarrel.
>
>1980—Louise Maddocks.

The girls have also acquitted themselves well in School shooting competitions, having two places in the winning Blundell's team in the British Schools VIII competition, 1981.

Possibly this is the place to insert a rather quaint advertisement that appeared in the advertising section on the back pages of some editions of *The Blundellian* during the late nineteenth century.

>"OLD BLUNDELLIAN". A choice *English* perfume
>
>"The vertiable breath of the flowers of Devon" approved by
>
>H.R.H. the Queen of the Netherlands and
>H.S.H. The Shazada Nazr'ullah Khan.
>
>Invented at Lake's elegant Pharmacy, 7, Gold Street, Tiverton, Devon.

21
Customs and Traditions

"It is a Blundellian Tradition that the male must at all times be protected from the female."   A. R. B. Thomas

A QUAINT insight into some of the old customs at Blundell's are found in the early chapters of *Lorna Doone*, where R. D. Blackmore was actually recording what happened when he was there in the 1830's. "Sheep washing" is described in *Lorna Doone*:

"In the third meadow from the gate of the School, going up to the River, there is a fine pool in the Lowman, there the Taunton brook comes in, and they call it the "Taunton Pool". The water runs down with a strong sharp stickle, and then has a sudden elbow in it, where the small brook trickles in, and on that side the bank is steep, four or it may be five, feet high, overhanging loamily; but on the outside it is flat, pebbly, fit to land upon. Now the large boys take the small boys, crying sadly for mercy, and thinking mayhap, of their mothers; with hands laid well at the backs of their necks, they bring them up to the crest of the bank upon the eastern side, and make them strip their clothes off. Then the little boys, falling on their naked knees, blubber upwards piteously, but the larger boys know what is good for them and will not be entreated. So they cast them down, one after the other, into the splash of the water, and watch them go to the bottom first, and then come up and fight for it, with a blowing and a bubbling. It is a fair sight to watch, when you know there is little danger; because, although the pool is deep, the current is sure to wash a boy up on the stones, where the end of the depth is . . . but even the boys who hated it most came to swim in some fashion or other, after they had been flung for a year or two into the Taunton Pool."

One Old Blundellian commented: "It was a rough but very effective lesson."

Blackmore also describes the making of "Winkies" where "the

scholar obtains, by a prayer or price, a handful of saltpetre, and then with the knife, with which he should rather be trying to mend his pens, what does he do but scoop a hole where the desk is some inches thick. This hole should be left with the middle exalted, and the circumference dug more deeply. Then let him fill it with saltpetre, of save a little space in the middle, where the boss of the wood is. Upon that boss (and it will be the better if a splinter of timber rise upward) he sticks the end of tallow or "rats rail", as we called it, kindled and burning smoothly. Anon, as he reads by the light his lesson . . ."

The P.B. stones that Blackmore mentions with flooding traditions are now at the "new" School, and the holiday associated with the covering of these stones has now gone, along with the half holidays awarded when any of the Masters' wives had a baby—the latter tradition was somewhat overworked by the larger and younger teaching staff now at the School. Occasionally some famous Old Blundellian "breathing all his old affections for the scenes of his boyhood" could persuade a Headmaster to award a holiday, as did Temple when Bishop of London.

> Fulham Palace, S.W.,
> 16th June, 1887.

My Dear Headmaster,

I write in every capacity that can be assigned to me to get a favour from you.

I want a holiday for the boys on the 21st.

I entreat you as an Old Blundellian, as a Blundellian scholar of Balliol, as a Blundell's Fellow of Balliol, as a Governor of the School; surely the combined petition of so many, all of them Blundellians, ought to prevail.

Do.

> Your humblest servant,
> F. Londin.

For the record, it worked.

The "Ironing Box" is vividly described in the opening chapters of *Lorna Doone*. It consists of a triangular area of grass bounded by the cobbled paths which lead from the two porches of this Old School to the causeway, and it had several practical uses. In more tranquil moments, for the playing of quoits or putting the shot, yet it is really known best as a place to settle differences within a code of set rules, like that of a fisticuff duel usually on Thursday afternoons, such as described on the occasion of Jan Ridd's fight with Robin Snell. Parson Jack Russell developed his boxing skills there and we cannot find any record of Archbishop Temple ever actually repenting of his own liberal use of the facilities during his school days. T. D. Taylor records Temple advising him when Temple was a Monitor and Taylor a new boy in 1836, like some latter day Polonius to Laertes—"Avoid quarrelling, but if any boy attempts to bully you and hits you, stick up to them, and hit him again."

General Sir George Chesney, Chairman of the 1893 Old Blundellian Dinner, reminiscing some of the humourous accounts of the pugilistic contests of his own School days, remarked that he was not so sure that fighting was in those days so reprehensible as some people thought it must have been.

Fagging

Fagging seemed to develop in relationship to the senior boys' attempts to break the poor fare that especially prevailed before the repeal of the Corn Laws:-

". . . the big boys grew fastidious, and formed into small societies of clubs of four or five members, which supplied, each of itself, a tea-set and some plates, knives, and forks, together with a little capital out of which a store of tea and coffee was provided. These were known as 'drinking parties'. Whenever one member of the Club received a hamper, its treasures were placed at the disposal of the whole party, and its bacon especially was sent down in slices day by day to 'Old Mother Cop' at the gates to be fried. If she supplied a dinner-plate full of fried potatoes browned over, with the fried bacon placed on top, she charged one shilling for the dish, but if she simply fried the bacon and returned it on a hot pewter plate, she was content with the dripping fat. Mrs. Folland was an excellent cook. 'She dressed', said one of her clients, 'everything we could afford to get for breakfast, but nothing in my recollection was ever so good as the fried potatoes, and never since have I tasted that dish in such perfection.' "

A pupil of 120 years later would also claim that he had never tasted a "double egg and chips" quite like Clapps could provide during one of those rare Tiverton passes in the 1950's.

"The working of each of these Clubs was confided to a senior small boy or "fag", who was allowed by the Monitors, the custodians of order, to go into the kitchen and perform various jobs for the benefit of his employers. His chief duties were to see that the breakfast and tea tables were properly laid, the tea properly made, the regulation milk obtained, slightly in advance in the morning—cold; and that enough milk was obtained in the morning to serve for the evening meal. He had also to keep the services clean, and for all this he shared as one of the Club without being required to contribute towards its expenses. The situation of "fag" was eagerly sought after by the senior small boys. A fag who was dismissed for drinking out of the spout of the teapot after breakfast protested that the charge was unjust, for he had only poured the tea down his throat out of the spout. The plea, uttered with many tears, met no acceptance, his masters failing to recognise the distinction."

Fagging today more closely resembles that of 150 years ago then even of 30 years ago, as this first year scholar writes:

"This lasts two years for North Close, one year for Francis House, Westlake, two years, School House, one year, Milestones, one year, Petergate, two years, and Old House don't do any at all. N.C. does not allow personal fagging but others do with a fee of about £10 a term, e.g. Westlake. The jobs are usually delivering milk, yoghurt, and fruit juice to those who have ordered it. That is called 'Slosh' and is to be done before 7.20 a.m. 'Knobs Cupboard' involves collecting used milk bottles and emptying waste paper bins. The washrooms have to be cleaned between 6.15 and 7.15 p.m. as with changing rooms. 'Matron's Fag' involves bringing back supplies after breakfast and on Sundays collecting up dirty sheets. Papers have to be delivered to a few seniors before 7.15 a.m. and the corridors swept out at the same time. This is all done on a rota basis. That is all from N.C's point of view. Personal fagging is not allowed by the housemaster but still goes on, though not in such a big way."

He goes on to talk about tuck and other aspects:

"I think it is expected that a Junior brings back enough tuck to supply his senior's needs. Regular checks are made on tuck boxes to make sure that we haven't got anything we shouldn't have, and at the same time it is a nice opportunity to take food away. So the 'sprog' responds by hiding his food in places like hollow compartments under the cabinets of drawers, among clothes and in the pillowcases of pillows."

As for punishment:

> "House punishment for the prep-room is done on an odd-job system. A book is kept and if you do something wrong a certain number of odd jobs is put on in the book. If you make a cup of coffee for a senior, some odd jobs are taken off. If a big job has to be done the odd job book will be referred to and a person with a lot of odd jobs will be chosen to do it. School punishment is different. Sides are given. For bad schoolwork pink sides are given. For something like riding a bike in the wrong place, blue sides are given. (Blue sides are still given in houses, not only in school.)"

Flogging

"It is the privilege of Schoolmasters to lick creation, and it seemed to us that Dr. Richards (Rev. William Richards, L.L.D, Headmaster 1797) not merely licked his pupils, but in doing so beat all rivals out of the field."
—Artemus Ward.

Snell refers to lines, caning and the birch as "incident" rather than "custom", though they were an accepted part of the life of any similar establishment along with cold showers and Latin prayers.

Samuel Wesley (Headmaster 1733-1739) gives advice on corporal punishment in his poem *The Character of a Perfect Schoolmaster,* 1737.

> "He grieves that custom over-rules
> And keeps that whipping up in schools,
> Let wicked rods be thrown aside,
> And canes or ferrules applied,
> Or let each schoolmaster invent
> Some more ingenious punishment.
> For doubtless in bare skin to deal
> Appears but coarse and ungenteel.
> He never could be reconciled
> To "Spare the rod and spoil the child."

Banks comments, "Wesley, if report be true, taught as Busby (of Westminster) taught, and flogged as Busby flogged".

Jack Russell's memorable flogging by Richards, and the tradition of "Bring me a birch!" are mentioned elewhere. The Rev. Thomas Cross, the founder of Old House, and first School Chaplain, was described "As a teacher he was strict, very clear, and most unbending, a firm believer in stern and manual inculcation of Latin grammar and arithmetic (he would often cane half a dozen boys in one hour). His arithmetic teaching brought out really astonishing results..."

Up to the recent past Monitors had the power of corporal correction, yet contrary to outside beliefs, they exercised that right very judiciously and solemnly, recording carefully in a special book the date, the culprits name, his crime and the number of strokes given; all this was signed by the Monitor himself. Some of the embarrassingly not-so-old caning books have reached the archives of Brian Jenkins, senior history Master, and much of their contents must be regarded as highly-classified information, or possibly useful fund raising material.

1942——— 6 strokes for cutting a compulsory Chapel concert, and being found out (from the School House caning book.)

1954——— 4 strokes for publicly cheeking a House tie when only a first term study.

1954——— 4 strokes for behaving like urchins in the Dining Hall thereby polluting the name of the House..."

However, some incidents were not in camera. It would appear that the activities of an unofficial School Ornithological Society reached the National Press: *The Daily Mail, 1964.*

Well, Why *was* she asked to the fete?
Sir,
I am delighted that the powers-that-be at Blundell's School, Tiverton, Devon have vindicated Miss Sophia Loren so handsomely.

It is now clear that the caning of 21 boys who went to see an X-certificate film in which she appeared was not a punishment for watching the actress doing a striptease—but merely for the offence of breaking bounds.

How else can one interpret the invitation to Miss Loren to visit a fete at the school in June?

If she goes, as she has hinted she might, there will be no one breaking bounds on that day.

It is encouraging to think that schoolmasters are a little more human and understanding than they were in my day—and perhaps that they too are looking forward to meeting this glamorous and highly intelligent woman.

Or could it be that the invitation came from a not-quite-official source?

William Wright,
Manor Cottage,
Keyston,
Hunts.

The New Boys Test

There has been a custom for each new boy, after having been at the School for 10 days to two weeks, to enter the holy of holies, the head of House's study, and answer questions about his House in particular and the School in general, put to him usually by the Head of House and another Monitor. Systems varied a bit from House to House; generally during his preliminary "study" period the new boy would be excused fagging duties and would be personally coached by a senior fag, who had a vested interest in his charges passing, or else he would be subjected to the same punishment as the candidate in the case of failure. We are very grateful to Cedric Clapp (P. 1960-1965) for loaning us his original notes that he made as a new boy. As well as having to be able to recognise every House, Monitor and colour tie, and Old Boys' ties, every sports cap, every rugger sock, whether house, colts or field, by his first ten days, the candidate had to absorb such vital information as Clapp recorded when he first went to Petergate in 1960.

Head of House:-McPherson,
House Monitors:-Currie, Kemm, Ogden
Hall Monitor:- Candy

First Four:- A. Smith, Peters, Tarr, MacAdam
Last term first Four:- Paine, A. Smith, Harrison, Clifton
Head Fag:-Barker
Last Head:- Milde
Last Head of House:- Sampson
House Librarian:- Norrish
House Captain of Sport — Petergate
Fives   White
Shooting   Candy

Cricket	Ogden
Rugger	Coleman
Cross Country	Ogden
Athletics	Duckworth
Tennis	Adam
Squash	Duder
Swimming	Hippisley-Coxe
Chess	Kemm
Lord High Warden of Croquet	Codd

The Lord High Warden of Croquet.—*Brian Newton*

Lists of the inhabitants of each study and dormitory were included and certain details of the other occupants of the House were also noted:

The Matron is Miss Cecily Bailey. The last Matron was Miss Verina Barbara Reiter.

Mr. Francis' car No. is PDV 234. His children are Ann, Rosemary, Dorothy and Joan. Mrs Francis' Christian name is Mary . . . etc"

Certain details relating to other houses were also to be mastered.

House	Housemaster	Tutor	Head of House	House Colours	Magazine
W.	Mr. Parker	Mr. Batstone	Bradbury	Yellow & Black	Westlake World
P.	Mr. Francis	Mr. Brook-Smith	McPherson	Maroon & White	Beaver
N.C.	Mr. Beatty	Mr. Clough	Dare	L. Blue & White	Blue & White
M.	Mr. Clayton	Mr. Park	Fisher	L. Blue, D. Blue & White	Methoria
F.H.	Mr. Reichwald	Mr. Gettins	Bishop	Flame & White	F.H. Recorder
O.H.	Mr. McElwee	Mr. Evans	Cole	D. Blue & White	Magpie
S.H.	Mr. Chanter	Mr. Crowe	Stuart-Jones	Red, Black & White	Wall Mag.

Head of School:- Dare
Deputy:- Stuart-Jones

The new boys' method of listing the academic staff was practical, though seemed to differ a little to the system practised in the Public and Preparatory School Year Book.

Room	*Nickname*	*Surname*	*Subject*
5	Reggie	Gibb	Geography
8	Chris	Reichwald	French
9	Sammy	Burton	English
15	Buzz	Gettins	French
18	Tags	Silk	Chemistry
21	Laddy	Panther	Gen. Science

Etc, etc.

The Sports were also broken down into suitable headings.

School Captains and Masters—1960

	Captain	Master
Fives	Gill Smith	Reichwald
Shooting	Drewitt	Brook-Smith
Cricket	Beatly	Crowe
Rugger	Gane	Parker
Cross Country	Beer	Chanter
Athletics	Beer	Kiely
Tennis	Layman	Clough
Squash	Ross	Reichwald
Swimming	Chapman-Andrews	Biggs and Mundy
Fencing	Slee	McElwee
Boxing	Gane	Mundy & Atkinson

There were also other important people to consider:-

School Tailor is Mr. Elsworthy.
Mrs. Jennings runs the Tucker.
"Billy" Beale is the School Bursar.
Mr. Pilkington is the School Porter.
Miss Physic runs the Bookshop.
Mr. King is the head of Kitchen.
Lab. Stewards are Davy and Dawson.
H.M's Sec. is Miss Davis.
Groundsmen and Cricket Professional is Tom Jennings.
School Mascot is a squirrel, the squirrels in the School are:-
On top of the Gym, on the new block and top of West Window, also on the Corps Badge.

"And of all my recollections of former days there is none which stands out before me, and which occupies so strong a position in my memory, as the memory of the days I spent when I was a boy at Blundell's School, and in the town of Tiverton. I can't help wishing sometimes that some-one who had authority, and not only authority, but power to do it, would change me into a boy once more, so that I could go back to Blundell's School. I can't help a sort of feeling that there was a happiness in those days which has never returned after those days passed away."

Frederick Temple, Archbishop of Canterbury.
1896-1902
From his address to the Mayor of Tiverton, Oct. 3rd 1900

22
The Teaching Staff

I AM not certain whether an appreciation of the teaching staff should be included under the chapter headed "Customs and Traditions" or under "Sport". I am very aware that I have not focused nearly enough on these great men and even now, at this late stage, my tributes will be very inadequate. They entered the School usually with a good Oxford or Cambridge degree; whether or not they were thoroughly versed in up to date educational theories, techniques or psychology and so on, I would not know, and in any case, it did not matter, for they achieved amazing results through their teaching. But not only that, they fed into the School those other things that are so often difficult to quantify, yet so vital in the building up of character. They were so individualistic, so rich in character, yet not arrogant; men with such wide horizons of interest, yet totally dedicated to *their* school, as Blundell's became. The hours they gave the boys each week were well above the normal requested. One has only to read *The Blundellians* of the 1920's and 1930's where letters were frequently written to the Editor from sports captains expressing gratitude to masters such as R. G. Seldon (Master 1924-1964), that gifted and highly respected classics master who holds an amazing record, that of scoring a century and taking 10 wickets on the same day for Devon Dumplings against the Somerset Stragglers in 1929, and T. R. K. Jones (already mentioned) for those hours they "gave up" for extra coaching in the cricket nets or on the rugger field. In his well written book *Winning Rugby,* Richard Sharp pays warm tribute to the quality and dedication of masters such as C. H. P. Silk and 'Ted' Crowe in coaching rugby and also refers several times to Mr. Grahame Parker (Master 1946-1968) who was also in command of the C.C.F., geography master, Housemaster of Westlake and for a while followed R. G. Seldon as captain of Devon County Cricket Club.

". . . One of the reasons we enjoyed rugby so much (at Blundell's) was that we were coached extremely well. Mr. Grahame Parker was the master in charge and he was quite exceptional as a coach. He had the coach's supreme gift—the ability to bring the best out of his team. Certainly he inspired all of us, and defeat in a school match, although always bitterly disappointing personally, was made all the more acute by the fact that one had let him down".

The masters would liven up the School clubs and societies by their very presence and their colourful contributions to the debating society in particular in such debates as "This house believes the art of oratory to be detrimental to wise and just decisions", (1952) produced lively argument never to be forgotten.

But it wasn't only the hours they put in, it was also the years. E. G. Peirce, (Master 1899-1945) never really seemed to leave the School scene, even when Mayor of Tiverton in the 1950's. If one added up the years later, for example, R. G. Seldon, J. W. E. Hall, A. R. B. Thomas and W. F. Fisher (Woodwork Master from 1930-1981) stayed at the School (some of whom could easily have become headmasters somewhere is they had so wished), it would take one back to the Battle of Waterloo. There was E. W. Chanter who, after completing his stint as Housemaster of Milestones (1946-1958), moved across the road to serve an additional sentence as Housemaster of School House (1958-1971). There was Capt. G. L. Gettins, the French master, whose cartooning often served him well, and delighted others, in relieving the correcting of French papers. (Some of these cartoons are reproduced in this book by kind permission of Mrs. Gettins.) The following interesting aspect of Mr. Gettins character was included in a tribute to him by A. R. B. Thomas in *The Blundellian* of Autumn 1972:

". . . He also made ingenious toys, one of his best being a clock which signalled the hours in a remarkable way; a cowshed door opened, the farmer came out with a cow which he steered round the house into another shed (slapping it with a stick to get it in), while the farmer's wife came out to view the proceedings. When this marvel of ingenuity was shown to a local farmer, his only comment was 'Us doesn't knock our cows', which delighted Geoff more than the most fulsome compliment."

There was C. T. Reichwald (Master 1954-1980) who seemed so absorbed in cricket, Blundell's and his regiment.

Then there was Mr. R. W. Gibb (Master 1945-1963) the senior geography master and Housemaster of Petergate. He always seemed so very immaculate and even after a liberal use of chalk and duster in a lesson could still leave the classroom looking as if he had stepped straight out of Saville Row. Mr. A. N. F. Panther taught from 1951-1972. He would roar into the School on some powerful motorbike seconds before the final bell of chapel. He had a unique and memorable way of teaching general science that would leave the subject indelibly printed on a pupil's mind. (Incidentally the custom in the fifties of boys automatically diving for cover under their desks when this popular master applied a match to a bunsen burner stems from the time he presided over one of the most unforgettable demonstration on the making of gunpowder ever witnessed in a school laboratory).

Mr. S. H. Burton (Master 1945-1964), that gifted English master and author, former president of the School Literary Club and currently Vice President of the Exmoor Society, wrote also about Exmoor, and opened up a new world to many genuine country lovers. "A walk with S.H.B. (on Exmoor) is often to be a 25 mile affair. . . our longest was 33 miles", wrote one colleague of his in 1953. There was Mr. Francis Clayton, who still resides in Tiverton. In the days when Latin was necessary for Oxbridge entrance, Mr. Clayton was able to get through 'O' level even those reluctant scholars who privately lamented the fact that the Emperor Augustus had not banished Publius Ovidius Naso sooner and further. Mr. Clayton also presided over the School Gramaphone Club in those happy uncomplicated days before Hi Fi, tweeter, wow, and flutter. He also produced some excellent School plays, and his rich voice could reduce the room into fits of laughter when he took a comic role in a School Play-reading Society event. Bismark's foreign policy or the Balkan problems were made so interesting when explained by Mr. C. D. Beatty (Master 1944-1969) who also resides in Tiverton, and who had a wealth of mnemonics to assist the absorption of those facts which examiners demand (for example, I still remember the Bills passed in Gladstone's second term of office as, "Gladstone Made Three French Employers Educated and Reformed).

Yet in all these cases it seems that the right amount of authority and discipline were still very apparent, and boys were secure in that.

Last year I was privilaged to visit W. E. Lyons Wilson a month or two before he died. He was in hospital in Tiverton. When I asked a group of nurses where I could find him their faces visibily lit up and one quickly volunteered to take me to the man, who, by his very presence had brightened up the life of that ward, with his kind interest in people, his uncomplaining nature, and his fund of highly entertaining and well recounted stories. Then in his nineties but instantly recognisable, he was

42. The XV 1956. (Photo Chandler)

Standing
R. N. M. Paige (N.C.); M. M. Davies (F.H.); A. R. Tinniswood (S.H.); J. P. Hutchinson (N.C.); C. J. Morcher (S.H.); C. F. Tyler (F.H.); R. O. Baker (M.); M. H. Goss (O.H.)

Seated G. C. Reynolds (S.H.); H. C. Tilley (O.H.); R. A. W. Sharp (W.); N. Bourne (P.) Capt.; J. M. Beckingsale (N.C.); C. J. Higgins (M.); F. J. Davis (F.H.).

Not Included——R. H. Maxwell (F.H.); T. P. Burgess (W.)

43. Winner of the Rosslyn Park Festival Sevens, 1981.

P. G. Whitlock, R. Maltby, S. A. Watts, J. Massie, W. T. Carden
I. M. Brierley, R. J. Taverner, G. W. Watts
with Cardinal Hume who presented the Cup and Mr. T. I. Barwell, Coach. (Photo Ideal Mark).

44. Girls' Squash Team 1978.
Back row l. to r.: Arabella Dawkins, Catherine Webber.
Front row l. to r.: Charlotte McKinnel, Sally Duffus, Nicola Hardick.

45. Denny Dart U.S.A. A.F.S. Student at Blundell's finishing the Junior Russell 1980 *(Tiverton Gazette)*.

46. Senior Russell 1982 Lowman crossing *(Tiverton Gazette)*.

47. Russell 1982 Old Blundellian Challenge Race Nigel (Sam) Broad (F.H. 1974-78) and Martin Paine (P. 1958-62) demonstrate the art of running on water. *(Tiverton Gazette)*.

48. Vic Marks.(F.H. 1968-73) Somerset and England.

49. Mr. Mepham (director of Gray Nicolls) presenting the Trophy to Hugh Morris (W.) (Capt of England Schoolboys).

in complete command. On being asked after his health, he lightly dismissed that with "Very kind of you to ask, but actually I'm absolutely fine down as far the waist, but a bit slow from there on." He examined the sketches I had done with interest, making some helpful comments as to the placing of people and shadows. He was right of course, and I returned home to make the necessary alterations.

I often see A. R. B. Thomas. He has the looks and energy of a man 20 years his junior, with a lovely family around him. His two cats are probably more aristocratic that those two old feline warriors that 'graced' FH in the fifties. His days of jumping from the floor to the mantlepiece in the masters' common room in one leap may be behind him now—though it should be recorded that the mantlepiece retired first, when the common room was re-designed. But if my understanding of the verb to retire is what my dictionary seems to suggest, a verb implying withdrawal, retreat, to seek seclusion or to go to bed—then A. R. B. Thomas has not retired. He still plays chess, bridge and bowls. He is a very active and keen gardener, and sings along with his wife Liddy and daughter Susan, in St. Peter's Church Choir. He has written two books on chess, and recently completed one on John Wesley's visit to Ireland. He has also written a childrens story book, and to cap it all, he and Liddy won second prize in a competition organised by the Beaford Centre in 1976, with a duet they had composed, a jolly lively song about ancient men, of lions and tigers, of starfish and serpents, of monkeys and magpies.

From *Baby Baalamb gets into trouble* by A. R. B. Thomas

Blundell's Today and Tomorrow

by A. J. D. Rees, M.A. (Present Headmaster)

THE very production of this book has exemplified the dedication of Old Blundellians to their school. As Blundell's moves towards its four hundredth anniversary and we celebrate the hundredth anniversary of its move from Old Blundell's to Horsdon, so we are conscious of those elements of continuity and tradition which characterise the English public school. This unofficial history stimulates an unofficial analysis of where Blundell's is now, and where it may be going.

The combination of political threat and economic recession has led many people both inside and without the private sector of education to doubt the future of its institutions. The evidence is overwhelming that many thousands of parents do wish their children to come to schools like Blundell's, and that they are prepared to make quite dramatic sacrifices to make this possible. Indeed, one of the most daunting aspects of a modern Head Master's life is to be aware of the extent to which families have mortgaged themselves to send their children to the school, and one hopes fervently that the quality of what we do is sufficient to warrant such unselfishness. Those who mock or doubt the sacrifices of such parents are misinformed and prejudiced.

Would Peter Blundell or even Augustus L. Francis recognize the Blundell's of 1982? Blundell of course never knew Blundell's, but one imagines that he would have been happy with the achievements of Popham. Francis was the driving force behind the move to Horsdon and, despite the building developments of the last thirty years, he would recognize the external manifestations of the school. What both men had, and what the school needs today, is a vision which could be turned into hard reality. Blundell wished to educate the poor scholars of the town; today we continue to accept that responsibility and educate many young people from the Tiverton area, either free or at a significant fee reduction. Francis provided an old school with a new opportunity to develop and expand. Blundell's has taken the chances offered and today has the good fortune to possess an excellent range of buildings set amongst elegant lawns, extensive playing fields, and areas of woodland which add much to the character of the place. The road, which must have been a major attraction in the selection of Horsdon, is now a "holiday route"; fortunately the streams of tourists largely pass through in the school holidays, and Blundell's has learnt to live with the A.373. Government has now decreed the building of the North Devon Link Road which will take (or so it is planned!) the traffic swinging away down the Lowman. Readers of this book will have to judge whether there is a net benefit, for while we shall lose the traffic (or some of it), the glorious view of the Knightshayes hill across the valley will be destroyed by the developments in the Lowman valley made possible by the building of the Link Road. On the south side of the school the view of Newtes Hill is already sullied by serried ranks of bungalows, seemingly trying to reach the hill crest and flatter land above; on the north side before too long we shall see the plastic-coated steel of new factories and warehouses. Blundell's must be committed to the long-term prosperity and adequate housing of its local community, but we must be aware that there is a price (even the route of The Russell is to be shifted!).

Blundell's has no right to another hundred years at Horsdon, no right to see 2004 and four hundred years completed. Its place in the sun has to be worked for each and every day, its natural advantages of site and location being exploited in the context of acute awareness of what other fine schools are achieving. A Blundell's which sits back on its reputation will properly disappear, for reputation is a volatile thing, and complacency the certain killer. Public schools are well run; many have finer buildings or better locations than Blundell's. At a time when the trend is from boarding to day education, location on the edge of a small town is not the most obvious recipe for success. Large numbers of boarders are essential if Blundell's is to survive and, more importantly, thrive; and so a **major** element in the task of today's Head Master is to make frequent **visits** to prep schools, persuading them of the quality of our particular school, and stressing its accessibility to the major population concentrations of the United Kingdom (and, indeed, to those living and working overseas). Old Blundellians may raise their hands in horror—surely a fine school (their fine school), needs no such 'marketing', yet few of our potential parents know much of Blundell's and they have to be persuaded, quite properly, of the merits of sending their children to us.

The visitor tends to see the school as a collection of buildings,—and yet the character of the place depends on people—the staff and the fellow-pupils with whom one lives and works over the years. Blundell's is therefore not one school, but four hundred and fifty different schools—one for each of its pupils. A school cannot be all things to all men; indeed it should not be. It must recognize the wide variety of young people who pass through it, and carefully distinguish between those areas in which uniformity is properly desirable and those in which individuality should be nurtured to encourage the development of mature young men and women properly equipped to succeed.

Blundell's must continue to stand by the traditional virtues of honesty, integrity, courtesy, academic standards, discipline, and concern for the welfare of others. If that is traditional in the eyes of some critics, then so be it. Is there really any virtue in rudeness, selfishness or ill discipline? We do need, however, constantly to challenge the means by which we arrive at the ends we desire. Curriculum is not fixed, the pattern of games and activities will change, buildings will change their use, traditions and conventions evolve. A particular challenge is how we can add to the range of our activities, and thus to the commitments of pupils and staff alike, without injuring or diminishing those which already exist.

Areas in which I hope to see Blundell's take a key part in the coming years stretch across the whole range of educational responsibilities and activities. As far as the individual Blundellian is concerned, some of the changes will be almost unnoticed; others will clearly impinge on his life. I seek not to rank these developments in order of priority, and their achievement will depend upon planning, good fortune and the continuing commitment of friends of the school.

Recent developments in the Workshops point to exciting possibilities. Problem-based design and technology has been added to the excellent art work and cabinet-making. The Amory Workshops are crowded with young people producing a remarkable variety of objects—solar furnaces and solar panels, windmills, a shopper's car, radio-controlled camera-carrying kites, and silver marked with the Blundell's hallmark. Much of this work is being linked to more theoretical studies in the Science Schools, to community service work in Tiverton and to many other aspects of school life. We have hopes that we may be able to build a small factory attached to the Workshops; Blundellians would benefit enormously from the opportunity to design, manufacture and sell products. These developments should be linked to important work in the field of computing and electronics in the Science School.

Gornhay Farm has a fascinating location on the north-east side of the school. We hope to reopen the farm, with a possible emphasis on rare breeds, tree cultivation, and perhaps a fish pond. It may be possible to reopen the old mill leat and drive a variety of water-powered (and Blundell's-designed and manufactured) machinery. Paradise Wood can be carefully preserved as a nature reserve as part of this scheme. We thus further identify ourselves with our agricultural surroundings.

Sport has always been important in the life of Blundell's. While seeking to retain the quality of the best team and individual competitive sport, we see an increasing interest in recreational rather than fiercely competitive activity. Larger numbers wish to sail, canoe and camp; and our newly-acquired base on Dartmoor will facilitate this development. Our planned Sports Hall will enable us to combat the Devon weather and provide both the competent and the deserving with good sporting facilities. "Sport for All" is a good ambition.

Blundell's is a national school located in Tiverton. Our responsibilities to our local community have already been stressed. There is much we can do in the way of community service, not on the basis of self-conscious patronage, but as a result of a real concern for others and a careful analysis of what Blundellians can contribute. Much will come from taking Blundell's into the community—music and drama, for example, can brighten the life of the institutionalized elderly, as can the individual visitor. Computer programmes can be written for the handicapped child, wheelchairs repaired, furniture modified. The schools buildings and land can be made available to local groups; and joint 'town and school' activities can be given further impetus. The School must play a full part in local initiatives to bring employment to Tiverton, and relate these to its own actions as far as career advice for Blundellians is concerned. Schools need to look beyond their own bounds if they are properly to establish their young people in the real world.

Blundell's has a future, no one must doubt that. We need to have faith in the past and future achievements of the school; but remember that while faith may move mountains, a shovel helps. A proper mixture of perspiration and inspiration will maintain Blundell's as one of the finest schools in the country.

A.J.D. Rees

Article 13 of the United Nations Covenant on Economic, Social and Cultural Rights, which the British Government signed as recently as 1976, and which is subscribed to by every civilised country in the world, states that member governments, including ours,

"Undertake to have respect for the liberty of parents to choose for their children schools, other than those established by the public authorities, which conform to such minimum educational standards as may be laid down or approved by the state and to ensure the religious and moral education of their children in conformity with their own convictions."

Quoted in the prospectus of Shobrooke House Prep School, Crediton

Engraving by William Hogarth (1697-1764) For Blundell's "School Feast" 1727.

BIBLIOGRAPHY

'The Blundellian'. Various volumes.
Blundell's—a short history of a famous West Country school by F. J. Snell. Hutchinson & Co. Ltd., 1928.
Blundell's School Register, 1770-1812, H. M. Rankilor, 1892.
Blundell's Worthies, 1604-1904 by M. L. Banks M.A. Chatto and Windus, 1904.
Boy's Season Book by Thomas Miller, Chapman & Hall, 1847.
The Church in an age of revolution, Alec R. Vidler. Pelican 1961.
Diary of a Devonshire Squire 1844 by W. P. Authers (1982).
Donations of Peter Blundell and other benefactors to the Free Grammar School at Tiverton, by Benjamin Incledon Esq. 1792.
Early Associations of Archbishop Temple. F. J. Snell. Hutchinson 1904.
Encyclopaedia Britannica, 1961 Edition.
English Public Schools. Rex Warner, Collins. 1945.
Historical Memoirs of the Town and Parish of Tiverton by Martin Dunsford, 1790.
The Honeysuckle and the Bee, Sir John Squire. Heinemann, 1937.
"A Hundred Years of Rugger at Blundell's", by E. R. Crowe, Blundell's 1968.
Joyful Schooldays—A Digest of the History of the Exeter Grammar Schools, by Doris M. Bradbeer, 1973.
The Kings England—Devon. Arthur Mee. Hodders Revised Edition. 1965.
Lorna Doone, A Romance of Exmoor, by R. D. Blackmore, 1869.
The Life and Death of H. Rochester Sneath, Humphrey Berkley. Davis Poynter, 1974.
Memories of a Master at Blundell's School, O. F. Granlund, Blundell's 1937.
Memoirs of the late John Russell and his outdoor life, by E. W. I. Davies M.A. Chatto and Windus, 1902.
The Odes of Horace, translated by James Michie, Penguin 1967.
Old Blundellian Club Registers—Blundell's.
Old Blundellian London Dinner Speech A. R. B. Thomas 1975.
The Oxford Almanacs by H. M. Potter. 1974.
Parson Jack Russell—Frank S. Pepper, Swimbridge PCC 1981
Public and Preparatory School Year Book, A. & C. Black. 1980.
Punch, 1905, 1906, 1909.
The Register of Blundell's School Part I 1770-1882 by Arthur Fisher (J. C. Commin 1904).

The Register of Blundell's School Part II 1882-1932 by Allan Stanley Mahood (J. C. Commin 1932).
The White Rabbit, Bruce Marshall, Evans 1952.
Very Superior Men, Alicia C. Percival, Charles Knight & Co. 1973.
Winning Rugby, Richard Sharp. Pelham Books 1968.
Some Notes on Blundell's School, A. S. Mahood, Devonshire Association Transactions Vol. LXXXIV 1953.
The History of Tiverton by Lt. Col. W. Harding (1845).

INVICTIS PAX
1914 - 1919
1939 - 1945